TOXIC LEADERS

TOXIC LEADERS

WHEN ORGANIZATIONS GO BAD

Marcia Lynn Whicker

Quorum Books
WESTPORT, CONNECTICUT • LONDON

Library of Congress Cataloging-in-Publication Data

Whicker, Marcia Lynn.
    Toxic leaders : when organizations go bad / Marcia Lynn Whicker.
        p.   cm.
    Includes bibliographical references and index.
    ISBN 0–89930–998–4 (alk. paper)
    1. Leadership. 2. Executive ability. 3. Executives—Psychology.
    I. Title.
    HD57.7.W457   1996
    658.4′092—dc20   95–44311

British Library Cataloguing in Publication Data is available.

Library of Congress Catalog Card Number: 95–44311
ISBN: 0–89930–998–4

First published in 1996

Quorum Books, 88 Post Road West, Westport, CT 06881
An imprint of Greenwood Publishing Group, Inc.

Printed in the United States of America

The paper used in this book complies with the
Permanent Paper Standard issued by the National
Information Standards Organization (Z39.48–1984).

10 9 8 7 6 5 4 3 2 1

Contents

Introduction:
The Nature of Leadership

Leadership to organizations and society is the equivalent of sex appeal to the individual:

- It is hard to define.

- Generally, but not always, it makes people feel good.

- We know it when we see it.

- The quest for it is ongoing and eternal, since either consciously or unconsciously, our search for it permeates all human endeavors.

- The demand for it, as well as the willingness to talk about it, seem almost unlimited.

- Individuals in any setting either exhibit it or they don't.

- While some individuals are so remarkable that everyone agrees that they exude it, perceptions of who has it and what is good vary widely among individuals.

- Our concept of what is good about it seems partly rooted in biology and partly culturally defined.

- How some individuals pursue it and other individuals exhibit or exercise it is socially constrained.

- Our perceptions of who has it rarely undergo rapid transformations, but may nevertheless evolve and change over time.

While sex appeal leads to sexual intercourse, which assures the continuation of society through procreation and progeny, leadership leads to social intercourse, and also assures the continuation of society through proficiency and productivity. Each is indispensable for the perpetuation of the human race. This book is about the latter, particularly as it has been developed in modern organizations in the United States.

Leadership is elusive and enigmatic, just as it is enlightening and empowering. It is a bright light among human energies that sometimes, by its very intensity, casts a long and dark shadow. It provides a picture of humankind that simultaneously captures the passions, puzzles, and paradoxes of human interactions. Leadership both projects to the future and reflects upon the past. It bursts with possibilities, flaunts peculiarities, and occasionally defies probabilities. It includes everything, yet may be stripped bare to nothing. Leadership is timeless. It exists as long as we do. Without leadership, there are no organizations. Without organizations, there are no building blocks for modern society. Without society, there is no humanity. Without humanity, we cannot live.

Pigeon-holed away in our organizational cubicles and cyberspace, we have grown dependent upon leadership to connect us in ways that count. We are "hooked" on it to point the way to productivity and progress. Leadership is more addictive than heroin; its high, greater than cocaine; its hangover, greater than liquor. The greatest accomplishments and darkest passions of the ages are expressed today through our leaders. They form our blood lines to each other. As our nerves, they feel and taste what we do, only more intensely.

Leadership is a powerful force. Good leadership is pervasive, persuasive, and persistent. Bad leadership is poisoned with pedanticism, posturing, self-importance. Both good and bad, we long for the intensity of our leaders. Through powerful leaders, we become potent. Through their energy, we are reinvigorated. We soak up their vibrancy to show that we are alive. But typically, our love for our leaders is one-sided: their successes become our own, while their failures are theirs alone. The greater the adulation we have for our leaders and the higher our expectations of their success, the greater the potential hate we harbor when they fail. We can turn with speed-of-light swiftness, devouring those we created and raised to pinnacles few achieve. But leaders who are on a hell-bent path to personal glory at all costs can devour us. At its most primitive, leaders and followers engage in a dance of survival, sometimes working together to bring down a common foe, sometimes circling each other suspiciously in a clash over who is truly the leader of the pack.

Do we choose our leaders or do they choose us? It is a two-way seduction with both parties willing. In the end, few remember or care who made the first move. At every juncture there is a possibility of rejection—sometimes great, sometimes small. Sometimes we panic that our leaders will desert us. Other times we long for the day they will do so. Only rarely are we indifferent. Nor are our leaders indifferent. Our leaders almost always care about continuing in their leadership role, even if they have ceased caring about us, for we are as intoxicating to them as they are to us. If leadership is our elixir, power is their aphrodisiac. In the long-run leader-follower courtship, both get the lovers they deserve. In the short run, good deeds may go unspoken and good followers may get crushed.

At its best, leadership is uplifting, unifying, and unaffected. It brightens the spirit, emboldens the mind, and emancipates the heart. At our best, we are uplifted, harmonious, and courageous, more concerned with progress than pettiness. Good leadership is inspirational, and at our best, we are inspired to care about growing, each other, and the future.

But we may not always get the best. This book is about when we do not. It is about being trapped in organizations where bad leaders have seized control and are using their power in ways that spin those organizations into turmoil and decline. It is about why such leaders are driven to destructive actions and how to recognize them. It is about how to live with bad leaders in the short run so you can survive to live without them in better times.

This book explores both the highs that trustworthy leaders evoke and the lows to which toxic leaders cause us to plummet. And it offers a caution that bad leadership is addictive because the intensity of powerful leadership—both good and bad—is addictive. The organizational ravages of toxic leadership can be just as devastating as the physical ravages of toxic drugs. Finally, this book offers change strategies to reject toxic leadership, to restore productivity, and to place organizations that experienced toxic leaders on the path to collective health.

CONCEPTS OF LEADERSHIP

Leadership is both under- and overstudied. It is understudied because there is much that we still do not know about it. It is overstudied because much has been written, compared to other human energies about which we also know little. Yet the effort to think about leadership in a systematic and rigorous way has not been futile. A plethora of topologies and conceptualizations have resulted. Some focus on organizational leadership, while others focus on leadership in society.

Concepts of Society Level Leadership

Weber and Societal Leadership. Max Weber thought of leadership in terms of societal change, developing concepts of traditional, charismatic, and rational-legal leadership.[1] Traditional societies, less advanced and industrialized, had traditional leaders, whose authority rested on a long-standing belief in the sanctity of tradition and custom. Positions of leadership are often inherited through birthlines, and the personal and leadership roles of the leader are intimately intertwined. Often traditional leaders have substantial and sometimes absolute authority within their societies. Toxic leaders described in this book sometimes attempt to revert to the absolute power of Weber's traditional leaders.

Traditional societies are sometimes transformed into modern ones by charismatic leadership, which serves as a bridge between the two stages of societal development. Charismatic leadership is based upon devotion to a particular person, that is, the charismatic leader. The leader inspires devotion from his sanctity, heroism, exemplary character, and ability to tap long-thwarted emotional needs of followers. Charismatic leaders often head movements or revolutions that result in massive social change. We examine some toxic leaders, especially the street fighter, who at times exude charismatic qualities.

Modern societies most typically experience rational-legal leadership, which is based on the belief in patterns of normal rules. While transitions in traditional leadership occur through birth, transitions in rational-legal leadership occur through orderly rules and may be based on merit or decision criteria, such as majority rule. The rational-legal leader maintains a personal existence separate from his leadership role. Rational-legal leaders typically maintain organized administrative staffs to assist them in the complexities of providing direction within modern, complex societies. One of the toxic leaders we examine, the controller, overuses the rules that modern societies require.

McClelland and Societal Leadership. Unlike Weber, who defines leadership primarily in terms of societal characteristics, McClelland uses individual inner drives as the basis for his views. McClelland differentiates between individuals on the basis of their primary motivation and discusses three driving needs: high need for achievement, high need for power, and high need for affiliation. Leaders with high need for achievement are very task oriented, and desire esteem and respect. Leaders with high need for power seek compliance and deference from others, while those with high need for affiliation seek love, affection, and adulation. Within this book, bullies and controllers clearly have a high need for power. Busybodies and street fighters have a high need for achievement, defined partially as maintaining their organizational turf. Absentee leaders and enforcers are more likely to exert a high need for affiliation.

Despite the individual orientation of his classifications, McClelland uses these types to discuss leadership variations across societies and societal change. He develops operational measures of need for achievement and applies the measures to children's literature to identify the dominant leadership type and culture in societies at different points in time.[2] McClelland finds a positive correlation between increase in measures of need-achievement in the literature and spurts of economic growth and development at the societal level. While societies before and after periods of economic take-off may have a large percentage of leaders with high need-power and need-affiliation, an increase in the percentage with high need-achievement, reflected throughout the culture, is a prerequisite for nations taking greater charge of their economic destiny and more fully using their resources to develop.

Burns and Transforming versus Transactional Leadership. James MacGregor Burns has also theorized about societal leadership.[3] He uses Maslow's hierarchy of needs as the basis for his framework of transforming and transactional leadership. He draws from Maslow's notions that individuals progressed upwards through a hierarchy of ranked needs, from basic physical, safety, social, and esteem needs to self-actualization. In each case, once an individual obtains a particular need level, additional rewards or incentives at lower levels produce diminishing returns in satisfaction and motivation. Similarly, incentives at levels beyond that obtained by the individual were not particularly effective either. Burns posited that the role of the leader was to assist and motivate followers to move upward through this hierarchy. Burns argues that transforming leaders help their followers do this, while transactional leaders primarily focus on maintaining institutional processes instead of follower needs.

Transforming leadership may take several forms. *Intellectual leadership* links conscious purpose to values and empowers followers. Conflict becomes a tool intellectual leaders use to convert generalized needs into specific intellectual proposals. At various tension points within society, intellectual leaders may rise to articulate needs and link purpose to goals.[4]

Reform leadership, more than any other form, requires power resources, such as substantial finances and funding, vast popularity, a solid political base, and a grasp of political needs. Reform leadership also requires considerable political skills, such as an eye for opportunity, negotiating and bargaining skills, and finely honed abilities to persuade and respond in a reciprocal fashion. Reform leaders are constantly confronted with divisions within their ranks, as they must forge coalitions with allies who have a multitude of goals, some linked to reform and others not. Strategy is a major preoccupation of reform leadership.[5]

Revolutionary leadership occurs when leaders bring about not just the transformation of individual followers, but of an entire social system. They provide a vision of the future that propels the birth of the ideas underlying the revolution and often the revolution itself. This type of transforming leadership is all consuming, since revolutionary leaders must be totally devoted to their causes. They must be willing to demonstrate that commitment by devoting time, effort, and, at times, risking and even giving their lives to advance the revolution's goals. As the revolution unfolds, the political consciousness of both leaders and followers is expanded to new states.[6]

Closely linked to revolutionary leadership is *heroic leadership*. Heroic leaders arise within societies undergoing profound crises, when existing mechanisms of conflict resolution, including traditions, customs, and old ways of conducting affairs, have all broken down. With this breakdown, mass alienation and social atomization paves the way for heroic leaders, who are distinguished by their intense relationship with their followers. Heroic leadership inspires belief in leaders because of their personal attributes and characteristics, almost independent of their tested capacities, experience, or stand on the issues. Cast into an ocean of uncertainty as the social fabric crumbles, the masses are willing to believe that heroic leaders can overcome obstacles and crises. Mass support is expressed directly through votes, applause, and other signs of popular support, rather than indirectly through intermediaries.

In contrast to transforming leadership, transactional leadership facilitates the functioning of existing groups and relationships within society. Like transforming leadership, transactional leadership may take several forms. *Opinion leadership* conceives of leader and follower as exchanging gratifications in a political marketplace. Based on exchange theory, bargainers attempt to maximize their political and psychic profits. Relationships are necessarily short-lived, because conditions change, preventing the repetition of identical exchanges. This type of leadership is interactive, so that leaders communicate with followers in a manner likely to elicit follower responses, and followers respond in a manner likely to elicit future leadership initiatives. Opinion leadership is characterized by quick changes in style and mood, reciprocity, flexibility, and volatility of relationships. At times, leaders become so adaptable that they are hardly distinguishable from followers. Tasks performed by opinion leaders include arousing or mobilizing political opinion, aggregating and aligning it, and facilitating voting, or the conversion of opinion into decision.[7]

Group leaders in Burns's depiction of transactional leadership types are often bargainers and bureaucrats. Small groups are among the most durable social forms and rely heavily upon give and take among members. Small groups manifest a powerful sense of mutual obligation and a need for reciprocity. They develop strong tendencies toward conformity, but with the aid of transactional group leadership, the conformity and consensus performs a function of promoting group unity. The primary source of conflict within the small group is the affiliation of members with other groups. Bureaucratization, while on the surface antithetical to small groups, induces oligarchical power structures that ultimately lead to many similar behavioral manifestations. Leadership of political interest groups also falls into this category.[8]

Political parties derive their power from the capacities of *party leadership* at every level to identify and activate the wants, needs, and expectations of potential party followers. Party leaders must mobilize economic, social, and psychological resources to meet or promise to meet the needs of followers. Controls on party leadership are built into party rules and promote democratic and open procedures. Pressures of doing combat with competing parties for public attention and loyalty, as well as the enactment of party agendas, however, press parties toward strong leadership and even oligarchy. These pressures are particularly strong in multiparty systems, where interparty competition is often more fierce, and party leaders must move quickly to bargain and to form coalitions in the political arena.

Legislative leadership is, not always, but often transactional rather than transforming in nature. In legislatures, typically tried and true techniques for blending goals of members and various interests are used, including bargaining, reciprocity, and payoff, guided by the values of fairness, tolerance, and trust. To push legislation forward, leadership initiates, monitors, and follows through on completion of transactions. Legislative leadership also oversees disputes and stores up political debits and credits for future negotiations.[9]

Executive leaders, in Burns's view, compete in a more constrained and confined arena than legislative and party leaders. Executive leaders are distinguished by a lack of reliable political and institutional support, dependence on bureaucratic resources such as staff and budget, and heavy reliance upon their own talent, character, prestige, and popularity when dealing with political conflicts. Executive leadership must deal with conflicts which are rooted in technological forces and interorganizational in nature. Executive leaders also shape and mold public opinion in a manner beneficial to policy enactment. They use various types of power typically found in large, complex organizations, including legitimate, reward, punishment, referent, and expert power. The main determinant of how much power they have is the extent of their institutional and personal resources, including control of hiring, work assignments, job security, promotion, pay increases, suspending, and firing. Any action must be weighed in terms of costs to these resources, if executive leadership is wielded effectively.[10]

Concepts of Organizational Level Leadership

Downs and Bureaucracies. In his classic book, *Inside Bureaucracy*, Anthony Downs developed a five-category topology of leadership styles, each distinguished by their motives and scope of interest: zealots, climbers, advocates, conservers, and statesmen. Loyal to society as a whole, statesmen are excluded from the description of bureau life cycles, since their occurrence is rare and they have nonbureau bases of power.[11] The remaining four types of bureaucrats may be characterized by two dimensions—the scope of interest of the official (small or narrow versus large or broad) and the nature of the official's motives (self-interest versus mixed motives encompassing organizational as well as personal objectives).

Zealots, loyal to narrowly defined policies within the agency's original mission, are characterized by mixed motives and a small scope of interest. Zealots typically control an agency during its youth. Zealots may become toxic leaders when their zealotry for their cause pushes them to engage in destructive behavior.

Climbers pursue power, income, and prestige, and exhibit self-interested motives and a large scope of interest since they are more risk-taking and less preoccupied with maintaining the status quo than are conservers. Sensing opportunities for rapid career advancement as the agency expands and grows, climbers typically dominate an agency during its middle-aged years. Climbers are more likely to become toxic leaders than other Downsian types, as they often put self-interest equal to or above organizational goals.

Advocates are loyal to more broadly defined social functions, exhibiting a large scope of interest and mixed motives. Advocates may be present in the agency throughout the progression of the life cycle, but typically are found in new and middle-aged bureaus. Advocates are more likely to be trustworthy leaders, as they have a strong sense of duty and need to promote the organizational mission.

Conservers pursue personal convenience and security. They are distinguished by self-interested motives and a narrow scope of interest. Conservers typically dominate a bureau during its old age.

Maccoby and the Gamesman. Maccoby uses the relationship that corporate executives maintain with their followers and with their tasks to create a topology. The implied leadership styles in Maccoby's types have been incorporated into the prototypes of trustworthy, transitional, and toxic leaders described here. Two types of executives are more typically found in middle management: the *craftsman*, an independent perfectionist concerned with the quality of work and product produced, and the *company man*, loyal to the organization and concerned with security. The company man usually has a consensus leadership style. In earlier times, rugged individualism was more valued, and the *jungle fighter* often dominated top corporate leadership. This type of executive is power oriented, individualistic, self-made, and hard driving. The jungle fighter has a command leadership style. In recent times, the *gamesman* has become more prominent—a top executive who loves contests, but eschews rugged individualism and going it alone. The gamesman excels at putting together winning teams. Maccoby's gamesman has a coordinating leadership style.[12]

MacGregor, Ouchi, and Theories X, Y, and Z. Using the work of Abraham Maslow as a basis, MacGregor contrasted Theory X style management and leadership with Theory Y.[13] These theories of management, along with the more recent Theory Z, also embody the three leadership styles of consensus, coordinating, and command styles used in this book.

Operating with a philosophy of "sticks and carrots," Theory X managers assume that employees are motivated by economic means alone, and must be directed and guided to achieve organizational goals through rewards and punishments. This approach also assumes that workers wish to produce as little as possible and are inherently lazy, self-centered, and resistant to change. Theory X managers generally use a command leadership style.

Theory Y managers are grounded in the humanistic school and, by contrast, assume that the proper role of management is to help employees fulfill their own potential in a way that is beneficial to the organization. Management creates opportunities for workers to help them achieve their objectives. Theory Y leaders use a coordinating leadership style.

Theory Z, sometimes called "Japanese-style management," extended Theory Y. Like Theory Y, it assumes workers are inherently motivated and eager to work. Unlike Theory Y, it assumes that workers can often provide much of their own direction, and should be integrated into management decision making through the introduction and use of quality circles, workers councils, and other participatory mechanisms.[14] Theory Z leaders use a consensus leadership style.

Kets de Vries and Miller and Organizational Instability. More closely related to this book's effort to describe toxic leaders and how to cope with them is the work of Manfred F. R. Kets de Vries and Danny Miller.[15] These authors apply psychological labels traditionally used to describe individual mental disorders to leaders at the top of organizations exhibiting dysfunctional characteristics. They contend that organizations begin to take on the personalities and dysfunctional behaviors of their top leaders.

Dramatic executives show tendencies toward self-dramatization and excessive expression of emotions. Craving attention and excitement, they incessantly draw attention to themselves and are narcistically preoccupied. They alternate between idealization and devaluation of others, showing an exploitative incapacity to concentrate or sharply focus their attention. They often appear superficial, suggestible, and risk relating to a nonfactual world. They take actions based on hunches, overreact to minor events, and generate feelings of use and abuse among colleagues. Both the bully and street fighter toxic leaders discussed in this book show dramatic tendencies at times.

Compulsive executives are perfectionist and preoccupied with trivial details. They insist that others submit to their way of doing things and see relationships in terms of dominance and submission. They lack spontaneity and the capacity to relax. They are meticulous, dogmatic, and obstinate. They are unable to deviate from planned activities, excessively rely upon rules and regulations, and have difficulties seeing the big picture. At times, they show an inward orientation, indecisiveness, and postpone tasks due to fear of failure. Of the toxic leaders discussed in this book, both the controller and the bully show signs of compulsive behavior disorders.

Feelings of guilt, worthlessness, self-reproach, and inadequacy are hallmarks of *depressive executives*. Depressive executives also feel helpless and hopeless at times and are at the mercy of events. They have a diminished capacity to think clearly, are indecisive, and show a loss of interest in and motivation to deal with the organizational problems at hand. These executives show little capacity to experience pleasure. At times, the absentee leader described in this book has some of the behaviors of this type.

Schizoid executives are detached and withdrawn. They are plagued with a sense of estrangement and lack of excitement and enthusiasm. They appear cold and unemotional. The sense of isolation workers under schizoid executives feel may cause them to lash out in bewilderment and aggression. Both enforcers and absentee leaders discussed in this book show some schizoid tendencies at times.

Suspicious and mistrustful of others, *paranoid executives* are often hypersensitive and hyperalert. They show constant readiness to counter perceived threats and are overly concerned with hidden motives and special meanings. They have an intense attention span, but are cold, rational, and unemotional in carrying out plans. Paranoid executives distort reality in order to confirm their suspicions, a preoccupation. Their defensive actions cause them to lose spontaneity. Plainly, bullies and at times enforcers and street fighters exhibit paranoid behaviors.

Whicker and Moore have applied the categories of Kets de Vries and Miller to U.S. presidents, finding that presidents typically at times showed both a primary and secondary neurotic leadership style.[16] For primary styles, Hoover, Truman, and Carter were compulsive; Franklin Roosevelt, Kennedy, and Reagan were dramatic; Eisenhower was schizoid; Johnson and

Nixon were paranoid; and Ford was depressive. For secondary styles, Hoover, Eisenhower, and Kennedy were depressive; Franklin Roosevelt and Ford were compulsive; Truman, Johnson, and Carter were dramatic; and Nixon and Reagan were schizoid.

Bing and Crazy Bosses. Jay Bing has also looked at dysfunctional executives within organizations, identifying five types of "crazy bosses": the bully, the paranoid, the narcissist, the bureaucrazy, and the disaster hunter.[17] The bully is vicious, the paranoid sniveling, the narcissist self-obsessed, the bureaucrazy alternatingly fascist and wimpish, and the disaster hunter always in search of the next train wreck. These types, while interesting, are not necessarily mutually exclusive. Unlike the categories of Kets de Vries and Miller, however, Bing's categories do not coincide with standard mental disorders, nor do they emerge systematically from well-documented leadership styles and from categories in Maslow's hierarchy, as do the toxic leader types discussed here. Nonetheless, Bing does recognize the same important problem addressed here: that bosses can be crazy, and when they are, most people in the organization as well as the organization itself are negatively impacted.

TRUSTWORTHY, TRANSITIONAL, AND TOXIC LEADERS

Part III of this book identifies three types of leaders and the personal characteristics and organizational impacts of each: trustworthy leaders, transitional leaders, and toxic leaders.

Trustworthy leaders are good, moral leaders. They can be trusted to put the goals of the organization and the well being of their followers first. They value self-esteem, the esteem of others, and self-actualization both for themselves and for their followers. Trustworthy leaders are green light leaders. Organizations with trustworthy leaders at the helm have a green light to progress in productivity and growth.

Transitional leaders are self-absorbed, egotistical leaders. They are neither uplifting in their long-term impact on others nor purposefully malicious toward them. Rather, they are focused on the approval of others and concerned with their personal role as leaders. Transitional leaders are yellow light leaders. Organizations headed by transitional leaders have a cautionary yellow light to growth. They lurch along at the mercy of the ebb and flow of external currents and trends.

Toxic leaders are maladjusted, malcontent, and often malevolent, even malicious. They succeed by tearing others down. They glory in turf protection, fighting, and controlling rather than uplifting followers. Toxic leaders are red light leaders. Their leadership plummets productivity and applies brakes to organizational growth, causing progress to screech to a halt. With a deep-seated but well-disguised sense of personal inadequacy, a focus on selfish values, and cleverness at deception, these leaders are very toxic, indeed.

This book explores the differences between good and bad leadership. The questions addressed are:

- What is the difference between good and bad leadership? Plainly in the short run, both types can be strong and commanding, or more participative and consulting, so leadership style should not be confused with whether the organizational impact of the leader is good or bad.

- What impact will toxic leaders have on your organization if they gain control? Through what stages of decline will your workplace and those in it likely pass?

- How can you recognize bad or toxic leadership before it has wreaked irreparable havoc on your organizations and personal lives?

- What makes bad leaders bad? Why do some bad leaders exude toxic characteristics while others exhibit a mixture of toxic and trustworthy behaviors?

- What can you do to protect yourself and your fellow workers if a toxic leader takes charge of the organization in which you work?

- And finally, how can you unite with others to adopt strategies to turn your organization around?

NOTES

1. Max Weber, *The Theory of Social and Economic Organization* (New York: Free Press, 1964).

2. David C. McClelland, *The Achieving Society* (Princeton, NJ: D. Van Nostrand, 1961).

3. James MacGregor Burns. *Leadership* (New York: Harper and Row, 1978).

4. Ibid., pp. 141–168.

5. Ibid., pp. 169–172.

6. Ibid., pp. 201–205.

7. Ibid., pp. 257–286.

8. Ibid., pp. 287–296.

9. Ibid., pp. 344–350.

10. Ibid., pp. 369–375.

11. Anthony Downs, *Inside Bureaucracy* (Boston: Little, Brown, 1967). For an analysis of these four bureaucratic types, see Marcia Lynn Whicker, "Recruitment Decision Strategies in Public Organizations: A Markhov Analysis," *Management Science and Policy Analysis* 5, no. 1 (Summer/Fall, 1987): pp. 64–83.

12. Michael Maccoby, *The Gamesman: Winning and Losing the Career Game* (New York: Bantam, 1976).

13. Douglas MacGregor, "The Human Side of Enterprise," *Management Review* 46 (1957): pp. 22–28.

14. William G. Ouchi, *Theory Z: How American Business Can Meet the Japanese Challenge* (New York: Avon Books, 1981).

15. Manfred F. R. Kets de Vries and Danny Miller, *Unstable at the Top: Inside the Troubled Organization* (New York: New American Library, 1987), p. 221.

16. Marcia Lynn Whicker and Raymond A. Moore, *When Presidents are Great* (Englewood Cliffs, NJ: Prentice-Hall, 1988), pp. 133–166.

17. Stanley Bing, *Crazy Bosses: Spotting Them, Serving Them, Surviving Them* (New York: William Morrow, 1992), p. 268.

I

THE NEED FOR
TRUSTWORTHY LEADERSHIP

1

The Social Costs
of Toxic Leadership

TOXIC LEADERS AS A SOURCE OF ORGANIZATIONAL DECLINE

The likelihood is great that almost everyone, at some point during the span of a thirty- or forty-year career, will work in an organization dominated by a toxic leader. Recognizing what is going on is the first step to dealing constructively with it. Analysis is no substitute for action, but action without it is part of what makes toxic leaders so malevolent and organizations go bad. If you have not had such a harrowing experience, no doubt one or more of your friends have.

In the United States, we dote on good leadership. Leaders are regarded as the source of all good and the root of all evil. Looking for a great leader to save us can, if carried to extremes, be a passive and unproductive approach to solving problems and assuming responsibility for our society. This book is not intended to expand the leadership cult and passive reliance on a super leader for salvation. Nor is it intended to do the reverse: blame leaders for the inherent flaws and limitations in us all. It is not intended to remove us from the responsibility of creating and contributing to responsible, productive workplaces and institutions.

Yet to ignore that bad leadership—toxic leadership—can be a major factor spinning an organization into decline is to ignore reality, that is, fiddling with imperial arrogance while the organizational city is burning. Thus, this book aims to shed some light on what was previously an underdiscussed and even undiscussed subject: sick organizations, what their impact is, and how bad leaders—toxic leaders—help create them. This book intends to provide support to all those employees suffering in silence in sick organizations. It

offers the hope to them that with perseverance, persistence, and understanding they eventually will work again in healthy organizations.

Toxic leaders are the opposite of trustworthy or good leaders. While
trustworthy leaders inspire their organizations toward greater progress and
productivity, toxic leaders inhibit progress and productivity. Toxic leaders
may hold formal positions of power, or may be informal leaders heading up
factions within an organization. Yet rarely do the heads of factions have
sufficient clout to push a whole agency or corporation into a downward spiral
without at some point assuming a formal leadership position.

Toxic leaders come in different forms and varieties; a paler version of toxic
leaders, transitional leaders, range from almost benign to more malevolent.
Some forms of toxic leaders are truly malicious. Sometimes they are difficult
to spot, masquerading, as they are wont to do, behind the trappings of
trustworthy leaders. Toxic leaders, especially early in a downward organizational spiral, may spew forth the rhetoric employees expect of trustworthy
leaders, attempting to camouflage their true intentions. Yet eventually, as
organizational decline becomes more pronounced, toxic leaders find it difficult to disguise their flaws and basic drives. As organizations plummet further
into chaos, infighting, and faction building, the true colors of toxic leaders
become apparent to all.

THE IMPACT OF DYSFUNCTIONAL ORGANIZATIONS
ON THE ECONOMY

Most organizations, like most people, go through good periods and bad
periods. For some, the fluctuations are small, dips are minor, and upswings
are equally short. But for others, the high and low periods last longer.
Organizations with strong leadership and a favorable environment may
experience lengthy good times, while those with weak or inappropriate toxic
leadership may experience lengthy bad times.

Organizational fluctuations in goal achievement, functioning, and efficiency are always a major concern of those employed by the organization, and
those who are its consumers, clients, suppliers, and investors. Yet, when a
large number of organizations plummet into malaise, the whole economy
suffers and declines. The impact of organizational turmoil and inefficiency
then extends beyond the neatly drawn formal hierarchical charts that reflect
chains of command and responsibility, and begins to affect the well-being of
the entire nation.

During the aftermath of the 1980s, with its go-go emphasis on success at
any cost, the whole U.S. economy appears to be teetering on the brink of
malaise and a long, slow decline. If the economy is the sum of the whole, and

organizations are components that make up the whole, then a large number of them—from private sector corporations to public bureaucracies and educational institutions—may be in turmoil as well.

In terms of sheer aggregate size and total purchasing power, the United States remains potent.[1] Its total economy toward the end of the twentieth century is almost three times the size of Japan's and twice as big as the combined economies of West Germany, France, and Britain. The collapsing Soviet GNP at that time, when translated into dollars even at a very favorable exchange rate, looked anemic compared to the U.S. economy. Yet the signs of decline are there for those who choose to look for them.

Indicators of Decline

Relatively Slower Growth in GNP. The U.S. growth rate in GNP has lagged behind that of Japan in recent times, and very far behind the growth rates of newly industrialized economies, such as South Korea and Taiwan.

Efficiency Gap. While the slower rate in GNP compared to that of Japan has occurred for the last two decades, a lagging U.S. growth rate in productivity has occurred for the past four decades. On average, the typical U.S. worker still produces one-third more than the typical Japanese worker, but this leading performance occurs only because Japan does very poorly in services and agriculture. The Japanese mom-and-pop stores greatly undermine service sector productivity, while five-acre rice farms hold down agricultural productivity. When these are replaced with larger department stores and larger farms, Japanese productivity per worker will escalate rapidly.

Furthermore, Princeton economist William Baumol predicts that productivity rates in the two countries will naturally converge, as the leader in productivity, the United States, uses up easy fixes and reaches the limits of economies of scale. Baumol notes the lagging rate of increase in productivity in the United States compared to Japan to bolster his claim. Thus, the downturn in the productivity rate is troubling, first, because it has slowed down at all, and second, because it is slower than that of Japan.[2]

Debtor to the World. During the 1980s and Reagan era, the United States slipped from being the world's largest creditor to its recent and unaccustomed role as the world's largest debtor. Every year its debts to other nations continued to mount. These debts manifested both trade and balance of payments deficits. During the 1960s and 1970s, imports to the United States grew rapidly, but so did exports to other nations. During the 1980s, however, export growth fell markedly, while imports continued to rise. By contrast, Japanese exports grew at double the rate of imports during much of the same time period.[3]

The results were predictable: by the early 1990s, the United States had an over $50 billion trade deficit with Japan. The Japanese success in building up such sizeable balances becomes even more pronounced and profound when the relative size of the two economies is considered.

The splurge in consumer, government, and business spending was made possible because foreigners were willing to lend the United States the money to run deficits, both trade and federal, year after year. However, fear that this willingness would eventually evaporate kept the United States looking furtively and continuously over its shoulder to see if the economic piper was demanding payment.

This imbalance in the growth of imports and exports brought about predictions of the end of Pax Americana, the period of U.S. dominance from the end of World War II throughout most of the latter half of the twentieth century. It brought about predictions of the rise of Pax Pacifica, in which Japan and other Pacific rim nations would grow to economic and eventually political dominance.

Technology Gap. Technology drives productivity. In the early 1990s, the United States invested about the same portion of GNP in research and development (R&D) as did West Germany and Japan, but, by virtue of the large size of the U.S. economy, its research and development investment in absolute terms is far greater than that of its major competitors. The United States also seemed to be doing comparatively well in R&D brainpower in terms of total numbers of research scientists employed.[4] Yet Passell and others have observed that the United States seems to be getting "less commercial bang for its research buck." When measured by the ratio of exports to imports, the United States used to lead in the world in various high-technology industries, but now lags behind West Germany and Japan. Trade balances of exports to imports for computers, business machines, scientific instruments, communications equipment, and electricity transmission equipment were all significantly less favorable for the United States than for its competitors in the late 1980s and early 1990s. In drug exports, the United States did exceed Japan but not West Germany. Only in the high-tech area of aircraft design and production did U.S. exports significantly exceed both Japan and West Germany.[5]

EXPLANATIONS FOR ECONOMIC SLIPPAGE IN THE UNITED STATES

Some have argued that the fault for this technology gap lies with the allocation of research and development dollars to military efforts rather than to exportable products incorporating high technology. These skeptics contend that the "trickle down" theory of benefit for R&D, where military R&D supposedly spills over and helps civilian R&D, is limited. Critics of military R&D note that high powered lasers for defense do not reduce automobile emissions or have much utility for pollution control devices, for example.

Others have argued that the U.S. focus on basic R&D has freed the Japanese to spend much of their development monies on commercial applications, an area in which they excel. The Japanese are internationally known for developing finely graded tolerances in the production of manufactured goods and for using these tolerances to facilitate quality control. As a result, in recent decades, their products have gained a world-wide reputation for being reliable, dependable, and well made, words that once, but no longer, were used frequently to describe American products.

The most obvious explanation for this relative slip, however, may lie within the heart of our organizations and institutions themselves.[6] MIT economist Lester Thurow has argued that the "benefits" the Japanese and Germans received from World War II were not the physical destruction of their aging industrial plants and equipment as many have contended. According to this argument, the destruction of aged plants forced our competitors to build new, more modern, and efficient ones, a "benefit" the United States, by virtue of winning the war and being separated by two oceans, did not have. Thurow believes this argument is false. He challenges manufacturers who believe this popular notion to go out and dynamite their aging plants and see what economic advantage they gain.[7]

Rather, the real advantage that losers of World War II gained in the subsequent race for economic prowess and hegemony was a forced reexamination of their organizations, institutions, social processes, and, most especially, their leadership. Having been led into disastrous conflict by bad or toxic leaders, the losers were forced to demand better leaders for survival— leaders capable of rebuilding organizations and institutions as well as physical plants and buildings.

The vanquished in World War II had no alternative: they simply had to change to survive. The toxic nature of those who led them to utter defeat was obvious. The need to create more effective and efficient organizations was plain. Consequently, social institutions, industrial corporations, government bureaucracies, universities and other educational institutions, as well as the working relationships between these major economic actors were all rebuilt from ground zero. The victor in World War II, the United States, had little or no pressure to change its leadership and social institutions. As a consequence of victory, the American way of conducting business and of production was canonized as the best if not the only way.

Both during and for some time after the war, the United States drew upon a phenomenal brain drain from Europe, resulting in the flight of many and the best of Europe's scientists to the United States. Before and during the war, this drain was prompted by the need to escape Nazi persecution and death. After the war, it was prompted by the appeal of our research institutions and universities. This brain drain gave the United States a considerable competitive advantage for several decades. During the 1980s, however, the competitive advantage the United States had obtained from the postwar brain drain had ended. Economic globalization was underway with a vengeance, undermining the hegemony the United States had obtained earlier on the basis of mass production for large, homogeneous, largely domestic markets.[8] And our leadership at all levels, in many instances in transition from trustworthy to toxic leadership, did not seem up to the task.

Toxic Leadership in the United States

Toxic leadership has affected all of our institutions during the last two decades of the twentieth century: In the White House, scandals from Watergate to Iran-Contra to Whitewater have diverted our national attention from more pressing needs. On Wall Street, merger mania, junk bonds, insider information, and illegal deals became the hallmark of the 1980s. In Congress, Abscam; side deals by Jim Wright, Speaker of the House; the peccadillos of Senator John Tower, whose womanizing and boozing prevented his appointment as Secretary of Defense; and the involvement of the Keating Five in the savings and loan mess are but a few instances reflecting toxic leadership. In education, excessive overhead charges at such prestigious universities as Stanford, Harvard, and MIT received publicity. Collusion among major private colleges in offering student aid violated antitrust laws. Professorial fraud on research grants plagued the scholarly community. In the financial world, the savings and loan crisis and the BCCI scandal are two of the biggest examples of toxic leadership. In religion, televangelists Jimmy Swaggart and Jim Bakker were shown to be hypocrites and to have misused funds. The space shuttle Challenger blew up before our very eyes, killing everyone on board, because attempts to draw attention to problems with the O-rings, the cause of the explosion, were silenced by toxic leaders. In political campaigns, negative attack advertising reached new lows during the 1980s and became ubiquitous.

The impact of these and other instances of toxic leadership has been to erode both our national spirit and our national productivity. To reverse this as we move into the twenty-first century, we must first understand who toxic leaders are, what tactics they use, what they represent, and how we might demand that trustworthy leadership replace toxic leadership. Not only do we deserve better: our economic future depends upon it.

NOTES

1. Peter Passell, "America's Position in the Economic Race: What the Numbers Show and Conceal," *New York Times*, March 4, 1990, pp. A4–A5.

2. Ibid.

3. Ibid.

4. Ibid.

5. Ibid.

6. See Michael Beer, Russell A. Eisenstat, and Bert Spector, *The Critical Path to Corporate Renewal* (Boston: Harvard Business School Press, 1990), pp. 179–208, for a discussion of the key role "revitalization" leaders play in restoring financial health to corporations. See also Paul Strebel, *Breakpoints: How Managers Exploit Radical Business Change* (Boston: Harvard Business School Press, 1990) for how effective managers may use economic breakpoints to benefit their organization, rather than resist inevitable change.

7. Lester Thurow, speech given at Midlands Technical College, Columbia, SC, March 1986.

8. Ibid.

2

What Makes a
Trustworthy Leader?

As the United States confronts considerable challenges in the future, the need for trustworthy leadership has never been greater.[1] The national agenda requires healthy organizations to meet these challenges.[2] Among these are:

- revising the educational system;
- integrating diverse ethnic and religious minorities and immigrants, and tapping the creative energies of each;
- resolving the disparity between the rich and the poor;
- developing and maintaining a viable health delivery system at a reasonable cost;
- restoring our technological edge in manufacturing;
- returning to the cutting edge in new technologies;
- making the economy competitive in the world by increasing exports and addressing the balance of trade;
- containing the federal deficit and national debt; and
- developing long-term capital and human investments to assure future economic growth.

These complicated, challenging, and difficult tasks can only be achieved if organizations in all sectors—public, private, and nonprofit—are healthy and performing to capacity.[3] Toxic leaders drive our organizations into decline.[4] Trustworthy leaders are needed to maintain their health and productivity.[5] But what does trustworthy leadership look like? What are its defining characteristics?

THE CHARACTERISTICS OF TRUSTWORTHY LEADERSHIP

Trustworthy leaders foremost must be able to inspire the trust of their followers, not just occasionally and in the short run, but consistently and over the long run. They do this by making decisions based on the interests of their followers and the well being of the organizations they lead. They lead out of optimism and hope, not out of pessimism and fear. Their values, while considering self, are not selfish nor self-centered. They appeal to higher levels of human impulses and motives.

At times, the characteristics good leaders must possess seem at odds with each other, indicating the inherent contradictions in the act of leading. Good leaders, then, must be jugglers, balancing a multiplicity of demands.

They must be

- communicative yet analytical;

- confident yet not cocky;

- cooperative yet competitive;

- determined yet flexible;

- capable of managing change yet stable;

- ethical yet close to their followers' values;

- optimistic yet realistic;

- outgoing yet reflective;

- people oriented yet task oriented;

- persuasive but not demagogic;

- risk taking yet not foolhardy;

- desirous of responsibility yet capable of saying no;

- visionary yet practical;

- patient yet persistent;

- empathetic yet able to make tough decisions;

- possessing a sense of history while retaining a sense of self;

- self-controlled yet expressive of emotion.[6]

Trustworthy leaders may have different leadership styles.[7] There is no single trustworthy-leader mold from which all who might be classified as such emerge. Some have argued that leadership is situational—what makes a trustworthy leader in one setting does not in others—and that the only common ingredient all leaders have is followers.[8] Yet despite their diversity, trustworthy leaders do share certain basic common characteristics (see Table 2.1).[9]

Knowledge of Themselves

Trustworthy leaders must know themselves and their own capacities. They must understand what their personal goals are, believe in their abilities to accomplish those goals, and possess the ability to prioritize among sometimes conflicting personal goals.[10]

Whether or not leaders are self-knowledgeable from an early age or acquire this insight later does not matter, according to Warren Bennis. What matters is that once self-awareness begins, it becomes a life-long process.[11] Self-knowledge helps trustworthy leaders maintain control of their personal lives. Unlike toxic leaders who are maladjusted and malcontent or who exhibit an arrogance not based in reality, trustworthy leaders are self-confident because they know the skills in which they excel and are aware of their weaknesses.

The inner confidence of trustworthy leaders helps them to maintain a sense of humor and a sense of proportion. This allows them to deal with stress dispassionately and diminishes overemphasis on self-importance. Effective trustworthy leaders are able to interject humor, even in very tense situations. Unlike toxic leaders who crack jokes at the painful expense of others, trustworthy leaders crack jokes at situations, or poke fun at themselves.

Table 2.1
Characteristics of Trustworthy Leaders

---

1. Knowledge of themselves
2. Knowledge of the external world
3. Self-motivation and drive
4. The ability to motivate others
5. Integrity
6. An ability to formulate persuasive, uplifting, and unifying messages for followers
7. Cultivation of talent
8. Vision

Knowledge of the External World

Both from formal education and from experience, trustworthy leaders develop a sense of history. They realize that history runs in cycles, and that patterns of events are likely to occur, both within organizations and within societies. Trustworthy leaders are constantly searching for knowledge of government, corporations, other institutions, and societies that extends beyond their immediate organizational settings.

Trustworthy leaders have good minds, which they carefully feed and cultivate to make their own mental resources personally useful and organizationally valuable.[12] Some are particularly bright and intelligent, absorbing and digesting information quickly.[13] Others digest and absorb information more slowly, searching for the deeper significance and patterns that link facts into coherent bodies of knowledge.[14] All trustworthy leaders, however, are skilled at integrating and synthesizing information from diverse sources to focus on critical issues in a timely manner.[15]

The best trustworthy leaders creatively recombine components to gain a fresh view of a situation or an insight into a new solution to a problem. While less creative individuals are only able to make minor modifications on existing solutions and paradigms, creative leaders are able to depart from tradition and to suggest new, bold, and innovative approaches to old problems.

Self-Motivation and Drive

Leaders must demonstrate a healthy lust for commitment, ambition, and drive to be in charge.[16] Trustworthy leaders have a high need to excel and achieve, but on their own terms and within the bounds of their integrity. This self-motivation drives trustworthy leaders to overcome obstacles. Trustworthy leaders are self-starters, taking the initiative rather than waiting for others to stimulate them to act. They have realistic ambitions, both for themselves and for their followers or group.[17] Exhibiting perseverance and stamina, trustworthy leaders are aggressive in their pursuit of goals, but not to the detriment of employees and coworkers. They balance the need to persist against resistance with the need to analyze and monitor the situations and trends that create the environment for change.

Trustworthy leaders know that they are constrained at times by the realities of compromise politics and the need to negotiate and build coalitions. Yet because their sense of priorities is determined by an inner drive and value system, rather than a situation, they advocate ideas and programs before consensus builds, rather than after opinions are set.

The Ability to Motivate Others

Trustworthy leaders shape the actions of others through communication and persuasion, encouraging people to work together to mobilize their interests in goals and ideals. When delegating tasks to others, they are able to convince subordinates and followers that their actions are important to the overall effort and goals. Trustworthy leaders care for their organizations, as well as for the employees in them.[18] This gives them credibility with followers and constituents.[19]

Trustworthy leaders work to develop and hone management skills, but their abilities go beyond and transcend the technical skills involved in daily management. These transcendent skills include the ability to manage conflict in a constructive manner. They know when conflict is healthy in helping to clarify group goals, and when it is not. They are able to bring about compromise between competing factions when compromise is needed. Trustworthy leaders, then, manage conflict and unify.[20] Toxic leaders divide groups and exacerbate conflict.

Integrity

Trustworthy leaders have a strong, deeply rooted sense of integrity, based on a highly developed value system that promotes the well-being of the group as well as the individual and seeks to lift individuals to higher need levels and aspirations.[21] Trustworthy leaders use the same value system for themselves that they apply to others. Further, the components of their value system are compatible with each other, creating a philosophy that involves goals broader than the mere pursuit of personal power.[22] Having such a philosophy creates humility and develops a perspective that individual ends are less important than the larger group purpose.

Integrity also involves character, empathy, and compassion, characteristics in limited supply or unavailable among toxic leaders. The trustworthy leader is able to identify with others and to understand why others react to specific circumstances. They do not become hardened to suffering or pain. Trustworthy leaders have the strength to ignore external pressures to subvert their value systems, remaining true to basic ideals despite peer pressures and surrounding conflicts.

An Ability to Formulate Persuasive, Uplifting, and Unifying Messages for Followers

Trustworthy leaders know how to formulate persuasive messages for their followers that appeal to higher level motives, not base motives.[23] Since trustworthy leaders personally operate with higher level motives, they tend to communicate those concerns and incentives to others.[24]

The messages of trustworthy leaders are relatively simple, conveying clear and limited priorities. They communicate hope and optimism rather than the pessimism and conflict conveyed by toxic leaders. The messages of trustworthy leaders cause people to band together, pooling resources, efforts, energies, and talents to produce a synergistic whole greater than the sum of its parts.[25] Unifying messages, strategies, and tactics are more persuasive in the long run than divisive messages. Even if toxic leaders are able to lead followers in destructive directions with divisive messages and tactics, the resulting conflict will ultimately exhaust even supporters of the toxic leaders. Employees will once again long for the uplifting, unifying messages of trustworthy leadership if given the option.[26]

Toxic leaders may gain temporary sway over followers by appealing to supporter greed and personal gain. Persuasive messages from trustworthy leaders may include elements of sacrifice for the greater good of the organization, but typically link appeals to sacrifice with promises of future gain. Encouraging a balance between immediate and future rewards is a function of trustworthy leaders.

Trustworthy leaders are not afraid to develop messages that incorporate change, for trustworthy leaders are not afraid of change. They do not embrace change for change's sake, but they do recognize that change is an integral part of personal and organizational growth.

Cultivation of Talent

Trustworthy leaders are constantly cultivating and developing talent, both their own and that of their employees.[27] They are interested in developing their own communication skills and learn to be good listeners. They become good communicators in various settings—one-on-one, small group settings, larger meetings, meetings with subordinates, meetings with high-level officials or board members, and large public gatherings. In each setting, they assess how best to get across the main points of their messages as quickly and effectively as possible. They sense when they are succeeding and are able to shift presentations in mid-stream when they are not.

Because they are confident in their own leadership skills, trustworthy leaders do not always have to be the one in charge. They establish an orderly decision-making process that functions well in their absence, recognizing that leaders who present themselves as part of an orderly decision-making apparatus are more persuasive than those who must always be personally in control.

Trustworthy leaders encourage others to develop their own talents: They suggest that employees continue their education, attend skills development seminars, and go to professional meetings where they will be exposed to new ideas and methods. Toxic leaders may try to stymie employee development, fearful that key employees will become more marketable and leave the organization.

Trustworthy leaders always have someone in training for most key positions, including their own, so they do not fear the loss of key employees, and they encourage key employees to stay by providing opportunities for them to fulfill personal goals while enhancing the organizational mission. They create a healthy, productive work environment that employees enjoy, using methods that encourage employee development and growth. By contrast, toxic leaders discourage anyone from learning their own job, fearing the competition and that they may be replaced. Toxic leaders also generally discourage employee development so that the organization will not have to deal with change.

Vision

Trustworthy leaders have a vision of the future—what the organization as well as individual employees could be.[28] They innovate.[29] They reach for the stars at times, but not too often, having their head in the clouds to see starlight better, but their feet remain firmly planted on the ground. Trustworthy leaders do reality checks periodically to make sure that their vision is in line with what is possible. They have staff and other employees who are constantly helping them challenge and refine their own vision of the future as circumstances change. The visions trustworthy leaders present are compatible with higher level human needs, as well as with what is possible.

Trustworthy leaders take the long-run view. When confronted with harsh environmental conditions or unexpected adversities, they will cut their losses and start again on more promising approaches, since they are not afraid to admit mistakes and to change aspects of their vision when they have to. Yet even then, trustworthy leaders do not lose sight of their long-run vision of what the organization could be.

TRUSTWORTHY LEADERSHIP AND MASLOW'S HIERARCHY OF NEEDS

James MacGregor Burns defines the best leadership, which he calls trans-formational leadership, in terms of Maslow's hierarchy.[30] Here, trustworthy leaders may be distinguished from their lesser transitional and toxic counter-parts by using Maslow's hierarchy (see Table 2.2). Psychologist Abraham Maslow devised a five-stage hierarchy of human needs and drives, where movement to the next higher level depends in part on satiation of a basic need at the next lower level.[31] An individual usually progresses through the need levels as he or she matures. The five levels in ascending order are (1) basic physical needs (food, water, shelter), (2) safety needs (protection from the elements and from human attack), (3) social needs (the need to belong to groups), (4) esteem needs (the need to gain the respect of others as well as to gain self-respect), and (5) self-actualization (the need to use one's talents to the greatest potential).

Trustworthy leaders typically operate at level four or five of Maslow's hierarchy. Level four is the level at which trustworthy leadership begins. Because trustworthy leaders have considerable self-respect, they are able to command the respect of others, and continuously work to expand that respect. Trustworthy leaders have no need or incentive to put others down or hold others back to enhance their own self-images, since moral leaders already have a healthy self-image. Their unwillingness to engage in the destructive games toxic leaders play or malevolent tactics toxic leaders use further enhances the esteem employees hold for trustworthy leaders.

The best of trustworthy leaders also operate at level five and are personally motivated by self-actualization. They want to use and expand their own talents, and as part of their leadership talent, to help others develop their talents to the highest possible degree. Level five trustworthy leaders do not just respond to the need to earn respect, even if decisions that command the respect of self and others are difficult and tough. While being concerned

Table 2.2
Leadership Types and Maslow's Hierarchy of Needs

Leadership Type	Maslow's Level
Trustworthy leaders	Level 5: Self-actualization needs Level 4: Esteem needs
Transitional leaders	Level 3: Social needs
Toxic leaders	Level 2: Security needs Level 1: Survival needs

about the feelings and sensitivities of others, level five moral leaders have moved beyond deep concern about what others think of their behavior.

Level five trustworthy leaders are driven to put their considerable talents to maximal use, so that they contribute as much or more to the organization and society as they take back. Level five self-actualization involves not an ethic of sacrifice, but an ethic of giving from the most fundamental part of one's being—one's talent.

By contrast, transitional and toxic leaders (discussed more fully in subsequent chapters) operate at lower levels in Maslow's hierarchy. Transitional leaders operate at level three and are preoccupied with social needs. Toxic leaders operate at level two, absorbed by security needs and occasionally may sink even lower to survival needs, when employment crucial to economic survival is threatened. Driven in their own lives by lower level needs, transitional and toxic leaders lack the capacity and reserves to uplift followers that trustworthy leaders have.

NOTES

1. John P. Kotter, *A Force for Change: How Leadership Differs from Management* (New York: Free Press, 1990). See also Gail Sheehy, *Character: America's Search for Leadership* (New York: William Morrow, 1988).

2. Bryan D. Jones, ed., *Leadership and Politics: New Perspectives in Political Science* (Lawrence: University of Kansas Press, 1989).

3. Peter Koestenbaum, *Leadership: The Inner Side of Greatness* (San Francisco: Jossey-Bass, 1991).

4. Manfred F. R. Kets de Vries and Danny Miller, *The Neurotic Organization* (San Francisco: Jossey-Bass, 1984). See also Manfred F. R. Kets de Vries, ed., *The Irrational Executive: Psychoanalytic Explorations in Management* (New York: International Universities Press, 1984), and Manfred F. R. Kets de Vries and Danny Miller, *Unstable at the Top: Inside the Troubled Organization* (New York: New American Library, 1987).

5. Gary A. Yukl, *Leadership in Organizations*, 2nd ed., (Englewood Cliffs, NJ: Prentice-Hall, 1989).

6. Malcolm E. Jewell and Marcia Lynn Whicker, *Legislative Leadership in the American States* (Ann Arbor: University of Michigan Press, 1994), pp. 17–18.

7. Elliot Jaques and Stephen D. Clement, *Executive Leadership: A Practical Guide to Managing Complexity* (Cambridge, MA: Basil Blackwell, 1991).

8. Gary Wills, "What Makes a Good Leader?" *The Atlantic Monthly* (April 1994), pp. 63–80.

9. Koestenbaum, *Leadership*. See also Marcia Lynn Whicker and Jennie Jacobs Kronenfeld, "Leadership Training Models in America," *Free Inquiry in Creative Sociology* 15, no. 1 (May 1987): pp. 35–39.

10. Thomas E. Cronin, "Thinking and Learning About Leadership," *Presidential Studies Quarterly* 14 (1984): pp. 22–34.

11. Warren Bennis, *On Becoming a Leader* (Reading, MA: Addison-Wesley, 1994), pp. 53–71.

12. Henry Mintzberg and James A. Waters, "The Mind of the Strategist(s)," in *The Executive Mind*, ed. Suresh Srivastva and Associates (San Francisco: Jossey-Bass, 1983), pp. 58–83. See also Fred E. Fiedler and Joseph E. Garcia, *New Approaches to Effective Leadership: Cognitive Resources and Organizational Performance* (New York: John Wiley & Sons, 1987), pp. 43–48.

13. See Robert R. Torbert, "Cultivating Timely Executive Action," pp. 84–108, and Chris Argyris, "Productive and Counterproductive Reasoning Processes," pp. 25–57, both in *The Executive Mind*.

14. Frank Friedlander, "Patterns of Individual and Organizational Learning," in *The Executive Mind*, pp. 192–220.

15. See Karle E. Weick, "Managerial Thought in the Context of Action," pp. 221–242, and Louis R. Pondy, "Union of Rationality and Intuition," pp. 169–191, both in *The Executive Mind*.

16. Wess Roberts, *Leadership Secrets of Attila the Hun* (New York: Warner Books, 1990), pp. 23–28.

17. Harold W. Reed, *The Dynamics of Leadership* (Danville, IL: The Interstate Printers and Publishers, 1982), pp. 208–211.

18. J. Donald Walters, *The Art of Supportive Leadership* (Nevada City, CA: Crystal Clarity, 1987).

19. James M. Kouzes and Barry Z. Posner, "The Credibility Factor: What People Expect of Leaders," in *Contemporary Issues in Leadership*, 3rd ed., (Boulder, CO: Westview Press, 1993), pp. 57–61.

20. J. Kevin Barge, *Leadership: Communication Skills for Organizations and Groups* (New York: St. Martin's Press, 1994), pp. 161–168.

21. Joseph L. Badaracco, Jr., and Richard R. Ellsworth, *Leadership and the Quest for Integrity* (Boston: Harvard Business School Press, 1989), especially Chapter 3, "Values-Driven Leadership," pp. 65–94. See also William D. Hitt, *Ethics and Leadership: Putting Theory into Practice* (Columbus, OH: Battelle Press, 1990), and Thomas E. Cronin, "Reflections on Leadership," in *Contemporary Issues in Leadership*, ed. William E. Rosenbach and Robert L. Taylor, 3rd ed., (Boulder, CO: Westview Press, 1993), pp. 7–25.

22. Henry P. Sims, Jr., and Peter Lorenzi, *The New Leadership Paradigm: Social Learning and Cognition in Organizations* (Newbury Park, CA: Sage Publications, 1992), especially Chapter 13, "The Ethics of Managing Performance," pp. 265–284.

23. Noel M. Tichy and Mary Anne Devanna, *The Transformational Leader* (New York: John Wiley & Sons, 1986), especially Chapter 5, "Creating a Motivating Vision," pp. 121–148.

24. Dennis T. Jaffe, Cynthia D. Scott, and Esther M. Orioli, "Visionary Leadership: Moving a Company from Burnout to Inspired Performance," in *Transforming Leadership: From Vision to Results*, ed. John D. Adams (Alexandria, VA: Miles River Press, 1986), pp. 95–104.

25. Tom Jaap, *Enabling Leadership: Achieving Results with People*, 2nd ed. (Brookfield, VT: Gower, 1989), pp. 144–145.

26. See Willem F. G. Mastenbroek, *Conflict Management and Organization Development* (New York: John Wiley, 1987), for a discussion of negotiation and conflict management skills that effective leaders use.

27. Gary A. Yukl, *Leadership in Organizations*, 2nd ed. (Englewood Cliffs, NJ: Prentice-Hall, 1989), pp. 132–137.

28. Warren Bennis and Burt Nanus, *Leaders: The Strategies for Taking Charge* (New York: Harper and Row, 1985), pp. 87–109.

29. Michael Robert, *The Essence of Leadership: Strategy, Innovation, and Decisiveness* (New York: Quorum, 1991), pp. 31–46.

30. James MacGregor Burns, *Leadership* (New York: Harper Colophon, 1978), pp. 112–119.

31. Abraham Maslow, *Motivation and Personality* (New York: Harper and Row, 1954).

3
Styles of Trustworthy Leadership

THREE LEADERSHIP STYLES

Trustworthy leadership does not come in just one form, but may assume different styles. Three leadership styles trustworthy leaders employ are command, coordinating, and consensus styles. The key to trustworthy leadership is not which of these styles is adopted, but rather whether the leader operates at higher level human needs, has a strong value system that is not self-centered and a sense of integrity, encourages employees to personally develop, is honest with him- or herself and with others, and has a vision of the future for the organization. Within those broad parameters, trustworthy leaders may have any one of three different styles. Indeed, the types of organizations in which leaders work may help define their leadership styles.

Toxic and transitional leaders may also adopt any of the three leadership styles. But toxic leaders act fundamentally differently from trustworthy leaders, even when they employ the same leadership style, because toxic leaders are insecure and are driven by a sense of personal inadequacy, a self-centered value system, and deceit. The difference between trustworthy leaders and toxic leaders, then, is not predominantly style, but rather the personal confidence, development, talent, value system, and character that the leader brings to the style.

These three styles of leadership closely parallel work done on human motivation. MacGregor contrasted Theory X with Theory Y leadership in bureaucratic settings.[1] Theory X leaders hold a worldview that employee and organizational goals are inherently incompatible, and the role of the leader is to use rewards and punishments to motivate followers to achieve organizational goals. This parallels the command leadership style.

Theory Y espoused the view that employee and organizational goals are potentially but not necessarily compatible, so leaders must structure situations to assure overlap. If leaders are skillful, followers, who are naturally motivated to achieve their own personal goals, will simultaneously achieve organizational goals. Theory Y parallels the coordinating leadership style.

More recently, Ouchi has espoused Theory Z management and leadership.[2] Theory Z leaders go beyond even the attempts of Theory Y leaders to minimize conflict between the organization and employees. They do this by allowing employees an active role in decision making and by encouraging their participation. In many respects, Theory Z resembles the consensus leadership style. (See Table 3.1.)

Command Leadership

Command leadership is strong and effective when employed by a trustworthy leader who possesses other-centered values and who operates at a high need level. Commanders, that is, trustworthy leaders with a command style, use meetings to communicate effectively and efficiently accurate information to employees. They use internal organizational norms of production to distribute raises, other monetary rewards, and nonmonetary favors.

Table 3.1
Trustworthy Leadership Styles and Behaviors

Command Leadership (Commanders)

1. Use meetings to disseminate information to followers.
2. Communication is predominantly downward.
3. Emphasize task achievement.
4. Distribute rewards on the basis of productivity.

Coordinating Leadership (Team Leaders)

1. Use meetings to both disseminate information to and solicit information from followers.
2. Communication is two-way, upward as well as downward.
3. Emphasize mentoring and development of follower skills.
4. Distribute rewards based on impartial external standards.

Consensus Leadership (Consensus Builders)

1. Use meetings predominantly to solicit information and generate a consensus.
2. Communication is predominantly upward.
3. Emphasize consultation and inclusion of diversity.
4. Distribute rewards so as to minimize differences and conflict.

Commanders may be perceived as taskmasters, but are viewed as applying the rules fairly and appropriately for the benefit of the organization as a whole. When employed by trustworthy leaders, the command style of leadership has several strengths. It is action oriented and emphasizes task achievement. Commanders develop a no-nonsense attitude toward work and productivity that frequently brings increased performance and results.

In contrast, toxic leaders with a command style may use meetings to disseminate misimpressions and even misinformation, embarrass employees, and smash dissent. Sometimes meetings are convenient mechanisms for encouraging or structuring conflict to the benefit of the toxic leader.

Toxic leaders with a command style are perceived as authoritarian and arbitrary. Command style toxic leaders run roughshod over employees' feelings. They create resentment and rebellion sooner or later among some subordinates.

Coordinating Leadership

Trustworthy leaders who use a coordinating style are team leaders. Their style is to coordinate activities through communicating a common vision. Trustworthy coordinating leaders use meetings to solicit information from subordinates that are used in making decisions that affect the organization, and as a forum for making suggestions to employees and work groups. Team leaders often use external criteria and norms (usually national professional standards) to distribute rewards and raises. Followers perceive this use of external criteria as impartial and fair. Trustworthy team leaders with a coordinating style are often mentors and teachers for subordinates within their division. They tend to emphasize continued development of follower skills and talents.

Under trustworthy leaders, coordinating leadership works well in complex settings where subordinates are highly trained and have individual areas of expertise different from the leader. Coordinating leadership allows subordinates the freedom to use their expertise and judgment in those areas in which they are knowledgeable, yet still provides guidance toward the overall organizational mission. Typically, team leadership also allows for a longer time frame needed to get results from innovations than does command leadership.

When a coordinating leadership style is adopted by a toxic leader, meetings are used to solicit information that can be used subsequently against employees and to feed information out selectively, if doing so bolsters the toxic leader's position. External criteria and national professional norms may be applied by toxic leaders arbitrarily to employees who have been given little or no chance to meet them.

Consensus Leadership

Trustworthy leaders with a consensus style use meetings to successfully resolve conflict and to create group unity. They minimize the differences in subordinate rewards and raises to reduce conflict that might disrupt consensus. They are consultative and may encourage employees having personal difficulties to seek counseling or other professional help. They encourage employees with lagging productivity and no professional skills to get them in order to keep raises and salaries of subordinates in line and minimize jealousy and dissent. They tend to encourage follower participation, knowing that followers will more readily buy into a decision in which they feel they have had input, thereby facilitating consensus building. The trustworthy leader with a consensus style resembles a knowledgeable big brother or confidant. Under trustworthy leaders, a consensus style incorporates everyone's opinions and avoids or reduces conflict.

Toxic leaders with a consensus style use meetings to bond with buddies in their own factions and to prolong conflict with and to ostracize others. Toxic leaders minimize the differences between employee rewards and raises to avoid penalizing members of their own factions and bringing unpleasant attention to declining individual and group productivity.

The toxic leader with a consensus style may be a drinking buddy or a consort in factional strategies. Under toxic leaders, the consensus style gives the opinions of inexperienced employees who support the toxic leader similar or even greater weight than the opinions of experienced and more skilled employees who may not support the toxic leader. Consensus style toxic leaders fail to recognize, reward, and cultivate merit even among supporters, but especially among opponents.

Leadership by Persuasion

Leadership by persuasion is a derivative of command, coordinating, and consensus leadership. Persuasion leadership combines those three leadership styles by using each of the three styles in appropriate settings. Persuasion leadership is a particularly appropriate style for top leaders.

Trustworthy leaders with a persuasion style use meetings for information flows in all directions. They use individual contributions to the group and value added to the organization as the criteria for distributing rewards. Trustworthy leaders with this style serve as catalysts and visionaries for followers and employees. Under trustworthy leaders, the persuasion style blends the best characteristics of the other three leadership styles.

The persuasion style can be tailored to specific circumstances, selecting the aspect or component that is most appropriate in any given situation. Its successful adoption depends on trustworthy leaders having great sensitivity, awareness of their surroundings, awareness of the feelings of followers, employees and audiences, and an ability to read their own personal impact on these groups.

Toxic leaders rarely have the skill to develop a persuasion style, as it is the most difficult style to develop. The persuasion style requires a wide repertoire of leadership skills and behaviors; a wide range of responses to subordinates, superiors, and others; and the discretion to know when to use each. Typically, toxic leaders stick to one style.

THE FIT BETWEEN LEADERSHIP STYLE AND WORK SETTING

In recent decades, a general trend toward more participative leadership styles has occurred, but command and coordinating styles are still used by trustworthy leaders with success. A linkage exists between leadership styles and work settings, that is, some work settings are more conducive to some styles than to others.

How well a style fits in a particular work setting depends on what the organization's goals are and how well the achievement of those goals can be measured. Organizational goals can be either narrow or broad. Measurement of the achievement of those goals can be either clear or vague, for reasons beyond the control of the organization and its leaders. (See Table 3.2.)

Command Leadership in Industry and the Military

In industry, the goals of the division or unit are specific: produce product X or service client Y within a specified time period. The criteria for measuring organizational success are clear: product X is or is not produced to a sufficient quality level and in sufficient quantity within the specified time period. Similarly, client Y is or is not served and satisfied with the service within the specified time period.

The most commonly used leadership style in situations where the organizational goals are narrow and the measurement of success in achieving those goals is clear is command leadership. Since the goals are well known and their achievement is readily ascertained, information directing task achievements flows more from above than from below. The command style is also characteristic of military organizations, which have a similar goal structure.

Consider the case of Lee Iacocca as a command leader in industry. The story of Iacocca's departure from Ford Motor Company to assume the helm at the financially ailing Chrysler Corporation is now part of national legend. Throughout his career, Iacocca had developed a reputation for drive, accomplishment, and focus on goals, exemplified by one of his major achievements, the Mustang.

Iacocca rose to become general manager of Ford Division before long-term tensions between Henry Ford II and Iacocca caused Ford to fire him.[3] Upon hiring Iacocca, the president of Chrysler made an analogy, comparing Iacocca to General George Patton. President Harold Sperlich discussed Iacocca's reputation for "inspiring the troops," for getting the job done, sometimes not by textbook methods, and for dominating most settings and people by virtue of personality and command of the situation.[4]

Likened to a field marshal, Iacocca's leadership style was to surround himself with loyal supporters who were bright but not yes men, "car guys open to new ideas."[5] His management techniques were described as "hard-nosed."[6] He controlled the personnel reporting to him directly by keeping tabs on them in his "black book," and instructed them to keep tabs on their subordinates in a similar fashion. Through the process of quarterly grading and reviewing of subordinates, Iacocca implemented his philosophy that "if you can't grade a man, you can't follow him at all."[7] Iacocca contended that his system of quarterly reviewing and reporting—a process that takes place annually in most corporations—forced managers to be accountable, rewarded productive employees, increased motivation, and stimulated problem solving. Nor was Iacocca afraid of wielding the ax when he felt it was called for. His command leadership lifted Chrysler from the brink of death by bankruptcy, just as earlier it had built up Ford.

Coordinating Leadership in Universities and Research Organizations

Universities and research organizations conduct research and development. The goals of a division or department in such a setting can be quite broad, especially for those engaging in basic scientific research. The goals may encompass such things as expanding the knowledge about cell immunology, or partial physics, or political revolutions, or just about anything. The division or department is creating something new in an area where the standards for judging innovation and creativity are ill defined. Hence, the organizational criteria for measuring goal achievement are vague.

Because the standards for judging the success of research and innovation are vague, judgments of employee success appropriately applied by the norms of good science often focus on the validity of the process employed in the conduct of research rather than on any specific research outcome or conclusion. Were the scientific method and standard operating procedures for scientific inquiry appropriately applied? By virtue of being new, the conclusion or finding cannot be known beforehand. Professional norms about the validity of scientific processes, however, are quite strong and may be based on peer review.

Consensus plays a role in this setting, particularly in establishing a peer consensus on the validity of research results. But peer review reflects a consensus of experts who may just as easily be located outside the organization as within it. The value of these experts in building consensus through peer review lies in their stature within the profession based on accumulated years of achievement, not in any particular position or title they hold within the organization at the time.

Despite the consensual nature of the peer review, the process of selecting peers appropriate for evaluation, as do many other aspects of university and research governance, requires collaboration, cooperation, and coordination. Thus, within universities and research organizations, leaders often adopt a coordinating style. Subordinates in this setting have professional reputations of their own, or at least the prospect of building their own reputations, and must be treated with respect. Further, these settings require considerable freedom and openness as well as individual judgment calls for innovation and creativity to occur. Yet the development of a coordinating common vision is necessary when the goals are broad and their measurement is vague.

A command leadership style would be too authoritarian for research and development settings, since command leadership works best when goals are clearly defined and measured. A consensus leadership style within the organization would not consider the many different professional accomplishments of various subordinates. It might also undermine professional norms if the opinions of new and relatively inexperienced subordinates are granted the same weight and significance as the opinions of long-term, more skilled subordinates with proven records in generating innovations and research results. A style that coordinates through vision and example draws on the considerable strength of followers yet provides overall guidance toward a common goal.

By virtue of the complex nature of the organizations they head, university leaders are often less known to the general public than the most famous of their professors who may win Nobel and Pulitzer prizes, large scientific grants, and public acclaim for intellectual breakthroughs. Some academic leaders, however, have provided a coordinating vision, not only to their own institutional constituencies, but also to broader groups beyond. Among these are Booker T.

Washington, who nurtured and developed the Tuskeegee Institute in Alabama as an institution of higher learning for blacks when many other opportunities were not available, and the University of North Carolina's Frank Porter Graham, whose position of racial tolerance and moderation challenged McCarthyism. Duke University President Terry Sanford similarly provided a voice of moderation against racial oppression, and Clark Kerr's leadership impact expanded well beyond Harvard during his presidency there.

Consensus Leadership in Government

In government, the goal of the agency or bureaucratic division may also be narrow—to produce a regulation to reduce the amount of fluorocarbons in the atmosphere to an acceptable level, for example, or to monitor or administer programs ranging from cleaning up toxic wastes to ensuring airport safety to policing the streets.

The criteria for judging success in achieving these goals, however, are vague. Governments primarily produce collective public goods rather than divisible private goods, often in response to crises and market failures. The outputs of government agencies are not processed through markets to gain a dollar value of worth, unlike those of corporations which are processed through competitive markets. This leaves the measurement of goal achievement vague. What is an acceptable level of fluorocarbons? What is enough cleaning up of toxic wastes, especially when the negative consequences of not doing enough may not emerge for years? How safe is safe enough for the streets and to what extent are the police to be held accountable for preventing the violent actions of others?

Because the criteria are vague, government leaders, unlike corporate leaders, cannot point to precisely measured achievements as proof of adequate job performance. If they are under attack from subordinates, other factions, or outside critics, the vagueness of the measurement of their achievements makes them vulnerable. Furthermore, these leaders often make decisions and implement programs in highly charged political environments. Public attitudes are often strongly antigovernment, based on the assumption that government bureaucracies are incompetent at best and evil at worst.

Thus, government leaders are likely to use a consensus leadership style to minimize the probability of attacks or sniping from subordinates, peers, superiors, and clients. If their superiors become unhappy with their performance, they can point to the solid support they have developed through consensus methods with their subordinates. The various levels of signatures often required in government for any decision seem like endless and needless paperwork compared to the number required for final approval in industry.

Elaborate layers of sign-off approval, however, are part of the process of documenting that consensus has been obtained.

Hillary Rodham Clinton's role in the development of national health care reform in the first year of the Clinton administration, though largely unsuccessful in achieving legislative changes, illustrates the consensus leadership style. Early in the first year of his administration, Bill Clinton appointed the first lady to head up the drive for health care reform. As the wife of the president, who was not receiving a government salary, her role was ambiguous. Her participation was challenged by some who felt her involvement was too great and even inappropriate. While much of the nation agreed that the system needed to be reformed to increase access and coverage, others disputed that there was a health care crisis, stressing the technological supremacy of American medicine and the adequacy of coverage for much of the insured population.

Assisted by Ira Magaziner, Rodham Clinton developed an elaborate task force to study the issue and make recommendations. From January to May 1993, five hundred experts were in almost continuous session, gathering in "clusters" and "working groups."[8] These experts sometimes met until the wee hours of the morning and on weekends, subjecting each other to presentations, papers, and slide shows. Before releasing the plan to the public, it was presented to contrarians and auditors for criticism. Modifications were made throughout the process, first to accommodate the opinions, assumptions, and contributions of policy experts, then to accommodate providers, including pharmaceutical companies, hospitals, and physicians. Efforts were also made to address the concerns of large and small employers, insurers, and consumer groups, such as the American Association of Retired Persons (AARP).

Even as the plan was announced, and subsequently defended by Rodham Clinton in impressive performances before congressional committees and public audiences, flexibility and the willingness of the administration to consider the concerns of others were stressed. Eventually, only universal access was defined as nonnegotiable with all other aspects of the plan negotiable; even the time frame in which universal access must be provided was left ambiguous to allow for the incorporation of concerns of key interest groups. The first lady's leadership in the development of health care reform was consensual, a style most often used in government where the goals are narrow in that they are policy specific, but the measurement of the goals is vague.

Leadership by Persuasion at Top Levels in All Organizations

Organizational environments, while distinctively different at middle and lower levels across industry, government, and research organizations, become

Table 3.2
The Fit Between Leadership Styles and Organizational Goals

Measurement of Organizational Goals	Organizational Goals	
	Narrow	*Broad*
Clear	Command Leadership (Industry and the military)	Persuasion Leadership (All organizations)
Vague	Consensus Leadership (Government)	Coordinating Leadership (Universities and research organizations)

much more similar at top levels. This similarity explains the mobility of top leaders among these environments.

At the top levels of all three types of organizations, goals are broad. Top corporate leaders are responsible for highly diversified company products, activities, divisions, and possibly international activities and exporting operations as well. Top level government leaders are responsible for a myriad of programs, cutting across many client groups and impacting on many segments of society. Top level university leaders must oversee such diverse schools and divisions as medicine, basic sciences, humanities, languages, and social sciences.

Yet, at the top of these organizations, the view of mission achievement is often clearer than it is at middle and lower levels, especially in government, universities, and research organizations. In government, universities, and research organizations, the view of goal accomplishment at middle and lower levels can be cloudy or foggy. At top levels, universities and research organization leaders want to support as many major research projects and produce as many major breakthroughs as possible. Corporate leaders want to produce the most favorable bottom lines as possible on income statements. At macro levels, top government leaders have social indicators (the crime rate, the morbidity rate, the quality of air index) that tell them whether or not conditions are improving in the basic areas over which they have responsibility.

Thus, the higher up a leader moves within any of these basic three types of organizations, the more likely that leader is to resort to a style of leadership that combines facets of the other three leadership styles. When dealing with subordinates in a crisis situation, strong, decisive command leadership may be appropriate. When dealing with a governing board, foundations, legislators, and other external actors, consensus leadership may produce the best results. When dealing with vice presidents, division heads, and other high level leaders with specialized expertise, leadership by example may work best.

Successful top level leaders, then, use leadership by persuasion to retain the flexibility they need to accommodate the diverse settings in which they find themselves. Usually toxic leaders and even some trustworthy leaders get stuck in one leadership style. They never make the necessary transition of broadening their leadership skills to include styles other than the one they initially adopted. Successful top leaders with a persuasion leadership style are a rare and special breed.

Perhaps more than in any other position of authority, presidents must develop a persuasive leadership style. Richard Neustadt noted that presidential power does not rest with official authority and job descriptions as defined in the U.S. constitution, but rather with the ability to persuade others to respond to presidential initiatives.[9] This power to persuade resides in an artful blend of official authority and unofficial personal characteristics and skills. Persuasive leadership includes but also supersedes official powers.

John Kennedy's leadership style illustrates persuasive leadership. During the thousand days Kennedy was in the White House, before his tragic death in Dallas, he blended leadership by command, consensus, and example into a persuasive style. His actions during the Cuban missile crisis and his reaction to the Sputnik threat with the "man on the moon" program and other initiatives represented strong, decisive command leadership. On the questions of civil rights and some social policies, Kennedy resorted to a consensus leadership style, seeking to include and incorporate concerns divergent from his own into administration plans. Previous long-term reliance on a family council of advisors had familiarized him with decisions by informed consensus of advisors, and his administration collected "the best and the brightest." In promoting the Peace Corps, youth activism, and national service—a philosophy reflected in his speech admonishing "ask not what your country can do for you, ask what you can do for your country"—Kennedy led by example. He proved capable of persuading the nation to elect its first Catholic and one of its most youthful presidents ever. Like many persuasive leaders, he integrated humor into his speeches and spontaneous responses to reporters, disarming them with light-hearted self-deprecation. His leadership stimulated a cohort of young people, including President Bill Clinton, to enter public service with missions of social improvement and reform. With his assassination, the promise of his persuasive leadership was cut short.

NOTES

1. Douglas MacGregor, "The Human Side of Enterprise," *Management Review* 46 (1957), pp. 22–28.

2. William G. Ouchi, *Theory Z: How American Business Can Meet the Japanese Challenge* (New York: Avon Books, 1981).

3. David Abodaher, *Iacocca* (New York: Macmillan, 1982), pp. 1–10.

4. Peter Wyden, *The Unknown Iacocca* (New York: William Morrow, 1987), pp. 1–22.

5. Ibid., p. 79.

6. Maynard M. Gordon, *The Iacocca Management Technique* (New York: Dodd, Mead, 1985), p. 11.

7. Ibid., p. 10.

8. Jacob Weisberg, "Dies Ira," *The New Republic* 210, no. 4 (January 24, 1994), pp. 18–24.

9. Richard Neustadt, *Presidential Power* (New York: John Wiley, 1960).

II

TRUSTWORTHY
VERSUS TOXIC AND
TRANSITIONAL LEADERS

4

Trustworthy versus
Toxic Leadership

To blame the decline of many institutions and organizations in the United States on bad leadership is to oversimplify the complex relationship between leaders and followers.[1] Followership is as important as leadership both in settings where individuals and organizations are lifted to higher levels and in cycles of decline. Yet the role of leaders cannot be overstated.

Leaders shape our visions of the possible and direct our energies toward it. When our visions are elevated toward higher achievements and our efforts are encouraged to be disciplined yet creative and innovative, much is accomplished. Trustworthy leaders provide us with this vision and direction. When our visions are reduced to viewing others within our own organizational houses as our greatest threats and our energies are directed toward defeating each other, much is lost. Toxic leaders encourage our baser instincts and release them upon each other to the loss of organizational productivity and individual self-esteem.[2]

Toxic leaders are the antithesis of trustworthy leaders. Toxic leaders may be technically skilled and quite manipulative.[3] They may have a strong sense of how to fight organizational battles. But the basic motive of toxic leaders is opposite that of trustworthy leaders.

Consider two leaders who greatly influenced the course of events in the twentieth century. One, Franklin Roosevelt, was a trustworthy leader, imperfect, as all trustworthy leaders are, but one whose primary focus was upon uplifting a population devastated by the Great Depression.[4] Roosevelt's values were democratic and Jeffersonian.[5] His methods were those of building coalitions, cajoling, designing programs to stimulate production and hire workers, and building a social safety net.[6] Popular with many but not all, his approach earned him the epithet of being "a traitor to his class." His politics were inclusive, not exclusive. His radio broadcast "fireside chats" reached out to people and inspired national confidence. Rather than scapegoat outgroups, he admonished the American people that all they had to fear was fear itself.

By contrast, Adolf Hitler defined toxic leadership. In an early speech, he declared that "whatever goal man has reached is due to his originality plus his brutality."[7] He had no use for democratic institutions, including free speech, free press, and parliament. He never trusted anyone, committed himself to anyone, or admitted any loyalty. His distrust of others was matched by his contempt for them. He saw men as motivated by fear, greed, lust for power, envy, and often mean and petty motives. Hitler viewed politics as the art of knowing how to take advantage of these weaknesses for one's own ends.[8]

Even though he spent many years drifting in Vienna as a failed art student scratching out a living at odd jobs, Hitler clung tenaciously to the notion that he was superior to others. He disliked the poor and downtrodden, but he disliked the working classes even more, for they threatened his notions of superiority.[9] He developed strong antisemitism that was originally sexual in its overtones, as he describes it in *Mein Kampf*.[10] He professed love for the German people but held them in great contempt. His bullying tactics, based in inferiority masked by a stance of public superiority and contemptuousness, ultimately resulted in genocide and mass destruction on a scale unprecedented. He was the ultimate toxic leader. Fortunately, most toxic leaders are not as destructive, evil, and devastating as Hitler, but he represents the extreme to which toxic leaders may go.

CHARACTERISTICS OF TOXIC LEADERS

All leaders, including trustworthy leaders, go through good and bad periods. During the good periods, trustworthy leaders are attentive to problems at work, on top of developing situations, sensitive to employee concerns, and articulate about organizational goals, strategies, and tactics for achieving goals. In good times, trustworthy leaders exhibit great skill at meshing employee goals with organizational goals so that both needs are met at once.

But even trustworthy leaders have bad periods. During these periods, they may be distracted from close attention to work by personal crises or problems, such as the illness or death of a family member, difficulties with a child, marital problems, or divorce. In bad times, trustworthy leaders may not be able to devote their normal energy to work, and their talents may temporarily be focused elsewhere.

What, then, specifically distinguishes a toxic leader from a trustworthy leader who is just having a bad period? Several factors differentiate the trustworthy leader in bad times from toxic leaders anytime. For the trustworthy leader, the period when attention is focused elsewhere and work is neglected or given short shrift is temporary, not a permanent on-going condition. These periods are infrequent and are largely caused by external events, which the leader cannot control.

Trustworthy leaders respond to such personal crises by resolving the crises, reconciling themselves to those things which cannot be resolved, or changing their personal status. Then trustworthy leaders once again have the energy available for leading at work, made stronger perhaps, or at least more sensitive to employees' personal problems, by having dealt with their own.

By contrast, distraction, poor production, and neglect of duty for toxic leaders result from internal tensions, conflicts, and problems. These internal tensions and problems are permanent, rooted in childhood and continued into adulthood, and arise frequently. Toxic leaders may be one of several types, but all toxic leaders share three defining characteristics: deep-seated inadequacy, selfish values, and deceptiveness.

Transitional leaders share these characteristics with toxic leaders, but in slightly less virulent forms. Transitional leaders differ from toxic leaders in that their selfish values are focused predominantly at Maslow's level three on social needs, rather than at Maslow's level two on security needs. Transitional leaders are, in essence, more benign forms of toxic leaders. Toxic leaders, by contrast, display the most malevolent forms of leadership. (See Table 4.1.)

Deep-Seated Inadequacy

All toxic leaders have a deep-seated sense of inadequacy, feel they are impostors and worry that someday someone will find them out. The reasons for this inadequacy vary across individuals and types of toxic leaders. Some feel inadequate because of unhappy childhoods. Others feel inferior from physical or intellectual limitations, both perceived and real. Yet this characteristic is the hallmark characteristic of toxic leaders: they all feel inadequate.

This strong sense of personal inadequacy has major consequences for the behavior and performance of the toxic leader at work. In its milder forms exhibited by some transitional leaders, this sense of personal inadequacy

Table 4.1
Characteristics of Toxic Leaders

---

1. Deep-seated inadequacy
2. Selfish values
3. Deception

---

causes the leader to merely withdraw from daily decisions and the on-going operations of the organization, lest close involvement and active participation in leadership reveal these weaknesses. In more severe forms, this sense of personal inadequacy causes the toxic leader to engage in frantic activity and to try to control every aspect of organizational activity, to prevent the toxic leader from being caught off-guard by an event or events he cannot possibly handle.

In an even more severe form, this sense of personal inadequacy results in a full-blown inferiority complex, where the toxic leader engages in posturing, puffery, and exorbitant bragging about personal achievements that are unfounded in performance. In its most severe form, a sense of personal inadequacy produces a malicious toxic leader who only feels competent and secure when tearing others down.[11]

Hitler's sense of inadequacy was rooted deeply in his childhood. He related poorly to his father (who died when Hitler was fourteen), a fact Hitler attributed to his father's resistance to his artistic ambitions but was more likely prompted by Hitler's poor performance in school. One of his school teachers from his early years later described him as lacking self-discipline, lazy, notoriously cantankerous, willful, arrogant, and bad tempered. Young Hitler was very hostile to advice or reproof while demanding unqualified subservience from his fellow students and fancying himself as their leader.[12]

Later Hitler tried to interpret the difficulty of his early years as one of poverty, but his family was reasonably well situated, and his mother received a pension that sustained them both after the death of his father, since Hitler showed little proclivity to work. He went to Vienna to study art, but failed the entrance exam into the Academy of Fine Arts twice. Nor could he enter the school for architecture as advised, since he lacked prerequisite credentials.

Hitler's shame over this caused him to avoid a hometown friend, his only close friend at that point, for five years. During those years, he lived an uncertain hand-to-mouth existence, partly due to his unwillingness to work steadily. He later described those years as the most unhappy of his life. Much was hateful to him—especially the whole ideology of the working class movement. He eventually blamed this ideology, which he believed corrupted nationalism and loyalty to the German state, on a conspiracy by the Social Democratic Party's leaders, and saw Jews as masterminding this conspiracy. Exorcising his personal inadequacy by tearing down others, he writes in *Mein Kampf,* "Was there any shady undertaking, any form of foulness, especially in cultural life, in which at least one Jew did not participate? On putting the probing knife carefully to that kind of abscess one immediately discovered, like a maggot in a putrescent body, a little Jew who was often blinded by the sudden light."[13]

Selfish Values

Leaders hold positions where their function is to guide, inspire, and set goals for the entire organization. Those who care about the organization, its mission, its workers, and its clients, should be the ones to lead it. Because of their deep sense of personal inadequacy, toxic leaders never develop personal values that give high priority to anything greater than their own needs.

All people, including trustworthy leaders, have personal needs, and at one level will pursue their own personal goals. To not do so is self-effacing and self-defeating. But trustworthy leaders seek out settings and organizations where their own personal goals are compatible with organizational needs. Trustworthy leaders place organizational goals high because they identify with the organization and the workplace mission. They perceive little or no conflict between what they must do as a leader and what they want to do as a person.

Some sacrifice is involved in being a trustworthy leader, but sacrifice is not the essence of a trustworthy leader's values and behavior. Trustworthy leaders are in sympathy with the organizations they lead. Just as good parents derive immense pleasure from the successes of the children they have raised, trustworthy leaders derive similar pleasure from the successes of the organizations they have shaped and led. They see no conflict between the organization succeeding and their own personal success.

Toxic leaders, by contrast, do not develop values that place organizational needs high. Their values focus on themselves, for they lack a sense of personal competency and are still trying to overcome their own sense of inadequacy. Their values are self-centered and self-promoting. They have not learned to expand their sense of what is good beyond their own restricted sense of personal well-being. Their perceptions of self-inferiority cause them to constantly compare themselves to others, rather than assess the skills of others and shape those skills into a broader whole.

Hitler's values were decidedly antidemocratic. His contrariness when young grew into absolute tyranny when he grew older. As he matured, the mental tensions and internal contradictions he felt got out of hand and, according to one biographer, became "the determinant of his whole being."[14] While in some ways he exhibited remarkable memory and bold imagination, he constantly underestimated and misunderstood moral forces with thinking in these domains that was "primitive and cranky."[15]

Remaining indifferent to women and to material wealth throughout his life, power became his consuming goal and mission. Hitler's arrogance was so extreme that he never admitted a mistake, even on a trivial matter and in the company of close associates. His arrogance grew into megalomania and hysteric rages. Hitler remained indifferent to normal human relations, one force that might have countered his fanatic nationalism and megalomania. He chose to remain single throughout his life, marrying only at the point of death. Family meant nothing to him, and he was estranged from his birth family. Of the six women who had some close human relationship to him, five either committed suicide or attempted suicide.[16]

Deception

Toxic leaders know or intuitively sense that they must deceive others about their selfish values and sense of inadequacy. Leaders are not supposed to have selfish values. Leaders are supposed to care about the organization, its mission, and its employees. Indeed, such caring is a necessary but not sufficient condition for true leadership.

But toxic leaders know they do not care about the organization. Toxic leaders care mostly about themselves and abating, soothing, and covering over their own insecurities and anxieties. They are shrewd enough to know they will be denied leadership positions which they crave to further abate, sooth, and cover personal inadequacy if they state their true motives. Thus, toxic leaders deceive others as to their true motives and intentions.

Deceit becomes the third defining characteristic of toxic leadership. Toxic leaders may differ in the degree and frequency with which they deceive others as well as the seriousness of the issues involved in deceit, but not in the fact that they deceive them. More benign toxic leaders need only deceive some of the time, such as, when conflicts emerge between their own insecurity and inadequacy needs and organizational goals. Then these toxic leaders will act in pure self-interest but state that concern for organizational goals underlies their decisions.

More malicious toxic leaders, however, engage in deceit most or all of the time. Malicious toxic leaders are driven to malign and tear others down in order to feel superior. They cannot reveal these motives to others for fear of being removed from leadership or attacked in self-defense. Thus, more malicious toxic leaders hide their intentions most of the time, since their true intentions are socially, morally, and organizationally unacceptable. They engage in a baser, more continuous, sometimes constant deceit that permeates the organization and destroys mutual respect and information sharing so crucial to efficient and effective organizational performance. But even the less frequent deceit of more benign toxic leaders is sufficient to destroy trust and produce an atmosphere of anxiety, suspiciousness, doubt, and malaise.

Hitler's deceit was embedded in his dual nature of projecting an image of a selfless leader, while being personally consumed with the drive for power. His deceit was the creation of a delusional world in which Germany dominated by inhuman rules and practices.[17] So great were his power needs and so persuasive were his skills that he was able to draw much of the German people into his delusional world of megalomania. In the end, he abandoned the nation in its hour of greatest need, deserting the people he misled, leaving them behind to confront the crimes for which he also should have answered.

NOTES

1. Joseph C. Rost, *Leadership for the Twenty-First Century* (Westport, CT: Greenwood Press, 1991), pp. 107–128, discusses the complexity of leader-follower relations in different settings.

2. See W. Richard Scott, *Organizations: Rational, Natural, and Open Systems*, 2nd ed. (Englewood Cliffs, NJ: Prentice-Hall, 1987), Chapter 12, "Organizational Pathologies," pp. 298–319, for the organizational problems that occur under poor leadership, including alienation, overconformity, uncertainty, unresponsiveness, and inefficiency.

3. Stanley Bing discusses the skills of various types of irrational executives in corporate settings in *Crazy Bosses: Spotting Them, Serving Them, and Surviving Them* (New York: William Morrow, 1992).

4. Philip Abbott, *The Exemplary Presidency: Franklin Roosevelt and the American Political Tradition* (Amherst: University of Massachusetts Press, 1990). See also Geoffrey C. Ward, *A First-Class Temperament: The Emergence of Franklin Roosevelt* (New York: Harper and Row, 1989).

5. Rexford G. Tugwell, *The Democratic Roosevelt* (Garden City, NY: Doubleday, 1957).

6. James MacGregor Burns, *Roosevelt: The Lion and the Fox*, vol. 1 (Norwalk, CT: Easton Press, 1956); also James MacGregor Burns, *Roosevelt: The Soldier of Freedom*, vol. 2 (Norwalk, CT: Easton Press, 1970).

7. Alan Bullock, *Hitler: A Study in Tyranny*, rev. ed. (New York: Harper and Row, 1962), p. 36.

8. Ibid., p. 37.

9. Ibid., p. 38.

10. Adolf Hitler, *Mein Kampf*, translated by James Murphy (London: Hurst & Blackett, 1939).

11. See Jay Carter, *Nasty People: How to Stop Being Hurt by Them Without Becoming One of Them* (Chicago: Contemporary Books, 1989), for a description of "invalidators," and how invalidators tear down the self-worth and self-esteem of others to build up their own. For protective strategies against verbal attacks and abuse from mal-leaders and invalidators, see Suzette Haden Elgin, *Success with the Gentle Art of Verbal Self-Defense* (Englewood Cliffs, NJ: Prentice-Hall, 1989).

12. Bullock, p. 27.

13. Hitler, p. 60.

14. Otto Dietrich, *Hitler*, translated by Richard and Clara Winston (Chicago: Henry Regnery, 1953), p. 11.

15. Ibid.

16. Ibid., p. 221.

17. Geoffrey Stoakes, *Hitler and the Quest for World Domination* (New York: St. Martin's, 1986).

5

What Makes Transitional and Toxic Leaders?

TRANSITIONAL AND TOXIC LEADERSHIP AND MASLOW'S HIERARCHY OF NEEDS

Trustworthy leaders uplift followers and, in doing so, inspire follower trust. They operate at high levels of Maslow's hierarchy, while transitional and toxic leaders function at lower levels. Trustworthy leaders are likely to be concerned with esteem needs (level four) and self-actualization and growth (level five). Their focus on these higher levels enables them to have the emotional energy and stamina to provide support to followers. They are able to develop an ethic of giving and support.

By contrast, the ethic of giving is alien to the value system of toxic leaders. Toxic and transitional leaders have not personally achieved Maslow's level four dealing with esteem or level five dealing with self-actualization and giving. Their deep-seated sense of inadequacy has arrested their personal development, so that they operate at levels two and three of Maslow's hierarchy. Transitional leaders focus on social needs and operate at Maslow's level three where their primary drive is to secure the approval and affection of others. Toxic leaders focus on security needs and operate at Maslow's level two, where their concern and need to protect turf, dominate, and control can prove very toxic, indeed.

Focused on social needs, transitional leaders are mostly concerned about belonging to groups, winning affection, although not necessarily respect, and being an important part of the organization in order to be assured of belonging. Transitional leaders will use their leadership positions to enhance the organization's goals only when those goals do not conflict with their personal needs.

Women are much less likely to be transitional leaders than are men, not by the grace of their comparatively overwhelming virtue, but because disproportionately fewer women hold top leadership positions. However, when women are transitional leaders, the busybody is a favored female type. Women with absentee leadership tendencies are not likely to assume formal leadership positions, since their inattentiveness will be interpreted as lack of seriousness and commitment, and powerful sponsors will not adopt them. Women are more likely to become controllers and even more so, busybodies. In the popular mind, gossip and rumors are associated as undesirable female characteristics. Women are given more popular leeway to assume the busybody role, in contrast to more overtly aggressive and hostile toxic leadership roles, and consequently, some do.

Unlike trustworthy leaders, transitional leaders have not achieved overall compatibility and harmony between personal and organizational goals. They will, when personal and organizational goals diverge, focus on personal goals by grandstanding, pursuing personal pleasures, limiting and restricting information, and making bad decisions that limit the future of the organization. Transitional leaders will let an organization drift into decline and, once in a downward spiral, may make decisions that continue its descent into dysfunction. Some organizations can reverse decline by neutralizing level three transitional leaders, at least in the less extreme cases. Other organizations under the guidance of transitional leaders sadly, in fact, meander into decline where toxic leaders emerge and productivity plummets.

Toxic leaders, typically more malevolent than transitional leaders, operate at Maslow's level two. They are obsessed with their own personal safety. In the context of modern organizations, this safety obsession is usually psychological, emotional, and functionally territorial rather than physical. Level two toxic leaders are constantly wary of attacks from others, and often perceive attacks where none exist. Toxic leaders adopt a military or warfare psychology, because they see their coworkers, subordinates, and superiors as the enemy.

Toxic leaders thrust an organization into decline even faster than transitional leaders. When a particularly powerful toxic leader is present in an organization, or when several exist simultaneously and negatively interact, disruption and dysfunctional descent are compounded and exacerbated. Recovery is more difficult and may not be achieved until toxic leaders have been removed from office and often from the organization.

Trustworthy leaders function at levels four and five in an ethic of honesty, encouragement of others, and giving. Toxic and transitional leaders function at levels two and three in an ethic of peer pressure, externally driven grandstanding, turf protection at all costs, guerilla tactics, and even paranoia.

The differences among the three are stark, and the different impacts they have on organizational performance is magnified by the scope of their power and control.

The "Mals" of Transitional and Toxic Leaders

Transitional and toxic leaders may be characterized by several "mals." Both are maladjusted, malcontent, and often malfunction; in addition, toxic leaders are malevolent and malicious at times, and are episodically hounded by malfeasance. In each instance, the characteristic is the opposite of what trustworthy leaders would exhibit. Each of the characteristics contributes to organizational decline.

Transitional leaders are concerned about their social needs. They have conquered their sense of inadequacy enough to not "see" an ambush or attack from coworkers, superiors, and subordinates lurking in every memo or decision. But they have not conquered it enough to exude the internally derived confidence and security that trustworthy leaders have. Transitional leaders still need constant reinforcement that they are okay by their participation and role in the group. They will bend their own sense of propriety to achieve it, as well as grandstand and puff up personal achievements at the expense of the organization. Of course, transitional leaders engage in deceit about their actions enough to generate distrust. Transitional leaders frequently exhibit three of the "mal" characteristics, especially being maladjusted and malcontent. The organizations over which they hold power may malfunction.

Toxic leaders manifest all the characteristic "mals" of transitional leaders—maladjusted, malcontent, governing organizations that malfunction—but toxic leaders operate at an even lower level, excessively focused on personal security because they feel so insecure and inadequate. They are consumed with building coalitions for making and fending off attacks and for making and preventing turf invasions. The most disturbed toxic leaders manifest signs of paranoia and see personal attacks and affronts lurking everywhere, even in normal daily operations. Toxic leaders hold hostile attitudes toward others and have a negative impact on organizations. They are often malevolent, finding evil everywhere, except, of course in themselves where it really resides. The meanest of toxic leaders are malicious, viciously attacking and trying to destroy others in a "destroy or be destroyed" mentality. This conviction that their survival depends on winning the battles they have conjured up in their minds and subsequently forced onto the organization sometimes convinces them that they must win at any cost, driving them into malfeasance to retain power.

Maladjusted. Transitional and toxic leaders are maladjusted to their positions and organizations. They are insecure about their own accomplishments, often with good reason, having avoided the personal risk, discipline, and hard work needed to succeed in earlier circumstances. Except for manipulation of others, their skills may be sub-par. They have assumed or seized power when others more qualified were available. Transitional leaders seize power when less qualified than others or even when unqualified in order to enhance their sense of belonging; toxic leaders do so to gain turf and preempt or prepare for attacks from others as well as to launch attacks on others. Both transitional and toxic leaders feel uncomfortable and insecure about this poor fit, try to repress acknowledgement of it, and deceive others about it.

Malcontent. All transitional and toxic leaders exude malcontentedness. They are continuously and constantly dissatisfied with circumstances, operations, and performances of others, projecting onto others their deep-seated discontent with themselves. They remain bitter about past personal failures. Toxic leaders especially are determined to make the world pay for egregiously overlooking or rejecting them in the past. Toxic leaders have been and are restlessly unhappy people.

Malfunction. Transitional and toxic leaders reign over organizations that begin, like themselves, to malfunction. Since these leaders are focused more on their own personal insecurities and mostly concerned about refuting or rebuffing their own and others' perceptions of their personal inadequacies, no one is focused on the interest of the organization: balance sheets and income statements that were once in the black turn to red; new and old product lines fail; and clients and customers turn away. Despite attempts to cover up malfunctioning, bad publicity spreads. Malaise, resignation, and even hopelessness emerge as productivity plummets. Employees are pitted against each other in an atmosphere of mistrust and malice, express anxiety about work, and spend more and more time on protecting themselves and infighting and less and less time on the mission of the organization.

Three additional "mals" are often exhibited by toxic leaders.

Malevolent. Because they are insecure and maladjusted, toxic leaders fear discovery that much of their leadership trappings are fake and their stated motives are false. They turn this fear away from themselves to generate fear of others. In doing so, many toxic leaders attribute evil to those they most fear and wish for evil to befall them. Such toxic leaders secretly cheer when coworkers, superiors, and subordinates fail, even when the well-being of the entire organization is threatened. The most malevolent of toxic leaders set out to sabotage others in the same organization.

Malicious. Toxic leaders are vindictive, wishing to inflict harm on others who challenge them. For some toxic leaders, this infliction of harm is intended as punishment and to assure that future challenges do not occur. For the most malicious toxic leaders, harm is inflicted even when there is no obvious factional or personal gain within the organization, purely for revenge. Rancor, malice, enmity, and spite are the trademark emotions of toxic leaders. The most malicious malign others both privately and publicly with great frequency and misrepresent reality to undermine coworkers.

Malfeasance. Haughty, arrogant, and insecure, toxic leaders sometimes cross the thin border between unethical or unprofessional behavior and illegal behavior. They may cross into malfeasance, committing illegal actions. They feel that normal rules for normal people do not apply to themselves and that the extraordinary evil of their opponents and/or their own extraordinary needs justifies extraordinary if shady or illegal actions. They feel they will not be caught and frequently they aren't, but sometimes they are.

TYPES OF TRANSITIONAL AND TOXIC LEADERS

The "mals" represent but a few of the differences between trustworthy leaders and toxic leaders. Yet toxic leaders often present themselves as trustworthy leaders. On the surface, they may seem charming, cordial, helpful, and even sympathetic. Initially, their baser characteristics encompassed in the "mals" may not be readily apparent.

Transitional and toxic leaders require close observation and time to discover their real motives and intentions. Across time, however, the discrepancy between the rhetoric of toxic leaders and the reality of their behavior and decisions becomes apparent. This discrepancy is rooted in the sense of personal inadequacy, selfish value system, and deceit that characterize all toxic leaders. Eventually, many or all of the "mals" will emerge.

Further complicating the quick and ready identification of transitional and toxic leaders is their diversity. Transitional and toxic leaders come in several varieties, each with their own peculiarities and obsessions. Like their trustworthy leader counterparts, transitional and toxic leaders may assume one of three leadership styles: consensus, coordinating, and command leadership styles. The trustworthy leader with a consensus leadership style is a consensus builder. The trustworthy leader with a coordinating leadership style is a team leader. The trustworthy leader with a command leadership style is a commander.

Unlike trustworthy leaders, transitional and toxic leaders who exhibit these three leadership styles do so from a base of deep-seated inadequacy, selfish values, and deceit. These leadership styles result in three types of transitional leaders, and three types of toxic leaders, each with a different style.

Transitional Leadership Types

Transitional leaders are the absentee leader, the busybody, and the controller. The transitional leader who is an absentee leader has a consensus leadership style. The transitional leader who is a busybody has a coordinating leadership style. The transitional leader who is a controller has a command leadership style.

Toxic leaders are the enforcer, the street fighter, and the bully. The enforcer is a toxic leader with a consensus leadership style. The street fighter is a toxic leader with a coordinating leadership style. The bully is a toxic leader with a command leadership style.

In some ways, trustworthy, transitional, and toxic leaders with the same leadership style resemble each other. The consensus builder, the absentee leader, and the enforcer, each with a consensus style of leadership, all seek direction and guidance from others. Consensus builders seek direction and suggestions from followers. Absentee leaders seek primarily affection and approval from followers. Enforcers seek the consensus and approval of those above them to whom they report.

The team leader, the busybody, and the street fighter, each with a coordinating style of leadership also resemble each other. Each of these leadership types both gives and takes direction from others. Each serves as a key focus of communication, with most key organizational information flowing through them. These leadership types differ, however, in the content of their communications and in their motives. They also differ in their impact on the organization, ranging from a healthy impact in the case of the team leader to a harmful impact in the case of the street fighter.

Similarly, the commander, the controller, and the bully all exhibit the command style of leadership and display some of the same behaviors. Each strives to be in command of their organizations and emphasizes directives to followers rather than input from others. Yet each of these styles differs in how command is exercised and what their personal motives are for exerting control over their organizations. Their impact on their organizations also ranges from the benign in the case of the commander to disruption, distress, and dysfunction in the case of the bully. (See Table 5.1.)

Each of the trustworthy leadership types has been discussed earlier in Chapter 3. A brief sketch of transitional and toxic leader types is given here. Chapters 6 through Chapter 11 provide snapshots of each of these harmful leadership types and suggestions for how to deal with them when you confront them in person in your workplace.

The Absentee Leader (Consensus Leadership Style). Disengaged and remote, absentee leaders are only tangentially involved in organizational decisions, manipulate symbols more than substance, and do not mind the organiza-

Table 5.1
Nine Leadership Types

	Maslow's Level of Leadership		
Leadership Style	Levels 4 & 5 Trustworthy	Level 3 Transitional	Levels 2 & 1 Toxic
Consensus	Consensus builder	Absentee leader	Enforcer
Coordinating	Team leader	Busybody	Street fighter
Command	Commander	Controller	Bully

tional store. Transitional absentee leaders seek the consensus of followers not about a vision of the organization, but rather about approval and affection for themselves. Absentee leaders are more mindless than malicious, but eventually create chaos and malaise from the turmoil and infighting perpetrated by underlings who are malevolent and who sense a leadership vacuum.

The Busybody (Coordinating Leadership Style). Energetic and constantly in motion, busybodies crave attention and affection, are sometimes fearful of alienating others, and specialize in manipulation of opinion and rumor mongering. These transitional leaders coordinate activities of followers by setting themselves up as the center of a communications network so that others must constantly turn to them to "tattle" on others. They often fail to make decisions that resolve conflicts among subordinates, assuring that the flow of complaints and information about conflicts and therefore attention received will be continuous.

The Controller (Command Leadership Style). Rigid transitional leaders as controllers are traditionalists and perfectionists. Their need to command others leads them to micromanage organizational affairs. Unlike street fighters, controllers lack the charisma to attract huge crowds and followings. Controllers manipulate followers predominantly through the control of information. They control by elaborate and selective use of bureaucratic rules, restricting and directing information to command the attention and obedience of followers.

Toxic Leadership Types

The Enforcer (Consensus Leadership Style). Subservient and often second-in-command, enforcers are toxic leaders who need hierarchy, certainty, and money, and who echo the toxic leadership styles of those to whom they attach themselves and support. They seek consensus with the leaders to whom they report, often other toxic and transitional leaders, rather than with followers. Enforcers rarely achieve dominance in an organization but are instrumental to the success of others, especially street fighters, bullies, and absentee leaders.

The Street Fighter (Coordinating Leadership Style). Egotistical and often charismatic, street fighters are toxic leaders with a "king of the mountain" syndrome who are driven to dominate through gang politics. Street fighters operate on gut level survival instincts and on the principle of rewards and punishments for loyalty to their "gang," rather than to the organization as a whole. They coordinate through rewards and punishments and their competitive vision of winning at any cost. They solicit input from followers who can help attain victory, but readily smash any who challenge them or dissent. Street fighters can be generous to those who show loyalty but vicious, exacting swift retribution, to those who do not.

The Bully (Command Leadership Style). Bullies are very angry, pugnacious toxic leaders who are mad at the world and jealous of others who outperform them. They are driven to invalidate and tear others down in any setting, including and especially work. Bullies are bitter about past failures and denigrate others to feel less like failures themselves. Bullies control through a variety of means, including and especially inappropriate, angry, personalized outbursts that lash out with the force of an emotional tidal wave.

TOXIC LEADERSHIP AND THE ORGANIZATION

Can leaders change types? If an organization is headed by a transitional or toxic leader, is that leader likely to improve? It is possible for leaders to change types, but not likely. Especially unlikely is a large shift in either leadership style (from, say, a command to a consensus style) or in Maslow's level of motivation (from a level two focus on security needs to a level four focus on esteem needs or a level five focus on self-actualization and growth). Thus, the probability that a toxic bully will become a trustworthy consensus builder is almost nil. Some incremental improvements may occur that involve leadership style (from, say, a bully to a street fighter), or more modest improvements in Maslow's hierarchical level (from a street fighter to a busybody, for example). And toxic leaders almost never achieve persuasion leadership, the appropriate combination and selective use of consensus, coordinating, and command leadership styles that is so much needed at the top levels of organizations. What is more likely are regressions in leadership—movements in negative directions. Once an organization is in decline and a toxic culture has been created, pressures build up for leaders to slip into leadership types that are more negative in their long-run impact on followers' well-being and organizational productivity.

Whatever leadership style is adopted, each of the six types of transitional and toxic leaders has a distorting and eventually debilitating impact on the organization they govern. If left unchecked, or reinforced rather than rejected and rebuked, the impact of toxic leadership can be quite deleterious. When an organization falls under the control of toxic leaders, a downward spiral of decline begins. Organizations may be turned around at each stage of decline, but the further down the spiral an organization has proceeded, the more difficult well-intentioned rescue becomes.

Organizations in decline are marked by plummeting productivity as well as malaise and low morale. Several stages of organizational decline will be discussed in subsequent chapters. Each is wrenching to the employees involved and results in ever lower levels of productivity. With each stage, employees become less focused on the true mission of the organization and devote ever greater degrees of energy to surviving in what has become an organizational morass.

Organizations that have spiraled downward to the last stages of decline most likely have experienced more than one type of toxic leader. Even relatively benign absentee leaders, however, can cause precipitous decline by allowing and implicitly encouraging other types of transitional and toxic leaders at lower organizational levels to wreak havoc on organizational functioning and productivity. Once a cycle of decline and a culture conducive to toxic leading is established, it tends to be self-sustaining and attracts other forms of toxic leaders.

Toxic leadership is not the only pressure generating organizational decline. Economic conditions also have a significant impact. A shift from favorable to unfavorable economic conditions and an increase in environmental uncertainty will increase pressure on organizations and the likelihood that some or all of the stages of organizational decline will emerge. The shift in economic conditions may come from several sources: a general recession, an increase in foreign competition resulting from globalization of markets, or the threat of a hostile takeover. In each instance, stress within the organization mounts and the flaws of toxic leadership, once acceptably disguised, become apparent and exacerbated under the resulting strain.

Organizations that were performing at an excellent level under favorable economic conditions drop to a mediocre lackluster performance when economic conditions become harsh. Similarly, organizations that were performing at barely acceptable levels in good times will likely spin into decline as conditions become more competitive and less favorable. These organizations will limp along as internal relations deteriorate along with the external environment. Some will barely endure and others will not survive.

When confronted with harsh and uncertain economic conditions, organizations with trustworthy leadership will rise to meet the challenge through innovation, resolution, and greater team spirit. Those with toxic leadership will waste precious time, resources, and energies fighting internally rather than strategizing and implementing new survivable, and perhaps superior futures. An organization in decline is like a train barreling out of control: bad economic conditions provide the rails that allow the organization to readily slip into decline, but toxic leadership provides the engine that drives it downward.

Like any sickness, organizational sickness resulting from toxic leadership, perhaps confounded by a downturn in economic conditions, can be overcome in most instances. But as with any illness, first, the patient must fight the sickness and become well before confronting in full force tasks of greater magnitude. Thus, an organization that has fallen into decline must heal itself by several strategies (to be discussed later) if decline is not too advanced. Then it can meet the challenges that caused the organization to decline in the first place.

Our entire economy is a complex mosaic of overlapping and many-faceted organizations. Most of our work is conducted in organizations. When any of these organizations suffers decline from toxic leadership, we may momentarily feel superior, especially if our own organizations are thriving and our current workplace is healthy and blessed with true leadership. But the reality is that when any of these organizations, especially large ones, suffers decline from toxic leadership, we all suffer directly or indirectly a loss in quality of life.[1] And no one is immune. The probability is high that throughout a lifetime of work, most people will run into a case of toxic leadership that will cause them personal pain, affect their career, and plunge their organizations into lower productivity and dysfunction. The lucky ones will experience this only once.

NOTE

1. Manfred F. R. Kets de Vries, ed., *The Irrational Executive: Psychoanalytic Explorations in Management* (New York: International Universities Press, 1984).

III

SNAPSHOTS OF
TRANSITIONAL LEADERS

6

The Absentee Leader

Thumbnail Sketch of the Absentee Leader (Consensus Leadership Style):
Disengaged and remote, absentee leaders are only tangentially involved
in organizational decisions, manipulate symbols more than substance,
and do not mind the organizational store. Transitional absentee leaders
seek the consensus of followers not about a vision of the organization,
but rather about approval and affection for the absentee leaders, themselves. Absentee leaders are more mindless than malicious, but eventually create chaos and malaise from the turmoil and infighting perpetrated
by underlings who are malevolent and who sense a leadership vacuum.

HALLMARK CHARACTERISTICS OF THE ABSENTEE
LEADER

The hallmark characteristics of the absentee leader are disengagement and
remoteness. Absentee leaders are emotionally distant from the work place and
frequently physically distant as well. At first glance, absentee leaders do not
appear to be a problem, in part because they often are not there. Yet this type
is commonly found in leadership positions in settings ranging from universities, where students cannot find their professors outside the classroom, to
middle and upper echelons of corporations, where executives are frequently
out "in the field."

Absentee leaders can even occupy the White House itself. Ronald Reagan,
a recent occupant of the White House with decided absentee leader behaviors,
took more vacation days from 1600 Pennsylvania Avenue than any president
in recent times, disappearing for days to his California ranch. He often left
work at 5 P.M., an unheard of time for other modern presidents who have

logged long and late hours. In his first term, Reagan delegated much presidential decision making about daily affairs and policy making to a troika of advisors, James Baker, Michael Deaver, and Edwin Meese.[1] Nancy Reagan greatly influenced his schedule and wielded considerable influence over his appointments to the White House staff and selection of close advisors.

Another famous absentee leader was Howard Hughes. Throughout his life, Hughes became increasingly eccentric and by the end, he not only eschewed any public appearance, but also was physically absent from his corporations and business, communicating only through associates. His top associate for a period, Noah Dietrich, reported that during a thirty-year period, Hughes visited Hughes Tool Company only once.[2] Indeed, the Internal Revenue Service became concerned that the absent Hughes was actually dead, and sought in vain to ascertain whether or not he remained alive and whether his multibillion dollar empire was being run by associates in his name.[3]

While other transitory leaders and toxic leaders may resist travel, absentee leaders roam restlessly around their territory, around the country, and if possible, around the globe. They rack up frequent flier miles regularly or, when possible, travel by corporate or government planes. While absentee leaders may profess deep interest in work, their I'll-go-anywhere-anytime-at-the drop-of-a hat attitude belies their verbal professions of commitment. While others undertake travel for pleasure and conspicuous consumption, absentee leaders travel to escape work. Howard Hughes, for example, often flew his own plane in the early years, and during periods of stress would disappear for days, flying around the Southwest. In later years, complete with entourage, he roamed from hotel to hotel in Las Vegas, Boston, and Hollywood.

Most absentee leaders are anxious to escape work regularly, since deep down, these transitional leaders often find their jobs, even the challenging work entailed in their leadership positions, laborious and boring. In many ways, absentee leaders resemble children who do not like school, and when sent home at the end of the day to do homework, will find any excuse to go out and play instead. Golf courses, conference resorts, tennis courts, ranches, and private homes of wealthy friends are frequent habitats for these transitional leaders. They are often seen at the openings of new plays and films, in new trendy restaurants, and on the golf course, rather than in the office with staff and other employees or with customers and clients.

Consider Samuel Pierce, the secretary of Housing and Urban Development (HUD) during the Reagan administration. Pierce, an absentee leader himself, presided over the biggest domestic scandal of the two terms.[4] During the investigations for fraud, kickbacks, and other corruptions at HUD under Pierce, Reagan did not visit the department once or speak in detail about how to resolve the situation, leaving the investigation and clean-up to others. The investigation revealed that Pierce had little knowledge of goings-on in his own department, spending his days, even while at work, watching television and whiling away time.

Others become absentee leaders when the stress level at work rises, producing concomitant increases in internal insecurity and doubts over abilities. Withdrawal, both emotional and physical, is the absentee leader's response. Howard Hughes had two major periods of withdrawal, detachment, and even mental collapse some contend, in response to increased stress levels at work. The first withdrawal, emotionally and physically, occurred shortly after he purchased two regional airlines and fashioned them into the major carrier TWA. The second major withdrawal occurred when TWA needed hundreds of millions of dollars to purchase a jet fleet, and Hughes had to seek external financing and consequently lose control of his airline.[5]

Yet another strategy employed by some absentee leaders is to diversify and dabble so much that they can never be one hundred percent in any location or activity and are absent by virtue of being spread hopelessly thin. Some of these diversifications are merely excuses not to focus and commit, and to play under the guise of work. Hughes's infatuation with and dabbling in Hollywood and film production may be classified as this, when his major areas of expertise and business were airlines, aerospace, military aviation, and electronics.

In one sense, absentee leaders are the most benign of transitory leaders. They are generally not personally malicious, and some do not care enough about work or their own image at work to become vindictive or vicious. They do not invest much of their own egos in work achievements or performance. Often absentee leaders are naive about bureaucratic politics associated with work, as well as the technical and substantive issues involved. Not liking "homework" and keeping the opposite in hours of workaholics, they do not advance substantially in technical skills and knowledge while on the job. What absentee leaders care about, instead, is developing a consensus among followers that they are nice and likeable.

Consider Reagan's claims that he was ignorant of the illegal selling of weapons to the Iranians to fund the contras in Nicaragua when Congress had withdrawn funding. His claims reflected the perspective of an absentee leader not on top of what was occurring in his own organization and naivete about how such actions might occur. Nor was Reagan always eager to pore over and study his briefing books. When approaching his first economic summit, Secretary of the Treasury James Baker delivered the briefing book to Reagan the night before, only to learn the next morning that Reagan had not even cracked it. When Baker inquired why, Reagan responded that *The Sound of Music* had been on television the night before.[6]

Nor did Reagan's knowledge of world trends and history advance significantly during his two terms, as throughout the duration, he continued to employ the technique of telling heart-warming, personal stories to illustrate a point, even after the particulars of several stories were found to be untrue. These stories did, however, serve the useful function of generating consensual affection among his followers.

Like all transitory and toxic leaders, absentee leaders have a deep sense of personal inadequacy. Unlike the most malicious toxic leaders who inflict this sense of inadequacy on others by "acting out," absentee leaders turn their sense of inadequacy inward and exhibit avoidance behaviors rather than aggression. Their sense of inadequacy is abetted by a remarkably low level of energy except when away from work and self-perceptions of a (sometimes real) lack of appropriate training for their current leadership position. These factors combine to prevent them from developing the confidence that, with effort, they could readily master technical and substantive details.

Because absentee leaders often do not work long and hard to compensate for weaknesses, and frequently start without much relevant training for their current leadership jobs, they sometimes appear to be slow or less bright than subordinates and peers. Their lack of interest in and familiarity with daily operational details, with technical aspects, and with substantive issues serves to perpetuate an image of absentee leaders who are not on top of things. Penetrating and incisive questions are not their forte. Cliches and common sayings are. In this way, they engender consensus among followers that they are likeable and non-threatening.

Unlike other transitional and toxic leaders who personally seize power, absentee leaders are likely to have been pushed into leadership positions by friends, funders, and business associates with ulterior motives. These friends and colleagues feel they can use the absentee leader to serve their own interests. Thus, the absentee leader often becomes a pawn of powerful interests who exploit the absentee leader's naivete, malleability, and desire to please. The absentee leader's insecurity and sense of inadequacy further reduces this transitional leader's already low tendency to question the motives and rationales of his sponsors.

Hughes, the eventual sporadic and absentee corporate leader, was pushed into heading up his father's enterprises by the premature death of both parents. Both had been vivacious and lively prior to their untimely demise. Hughes's beautiful thirty-nine-year-old mother entered a Houston hospital for minor surgery on her uterus and never recovered from the anesthetic, dying unexpectedly. His father was shattered, and Hughes, the boy, became withdrawn and lonely. Two years later, Hughes's father, having never shown any signs of ill health, was struck with a convulsion while having a meeting with his sales manager and dropped dead to the floor from a heart attack. The eighteen-year-old Hughes began a lifelong obsession with germs and became a hypochondriac, a condition that worsened with passing years. Hughes at the time was thrust into heading up his father's enterprises, but as a minor, was too young by Texas code to sign binding contracts. At age nineteen he had to make a special plea in probate court to waive age requirements and obtain legal permission to direct his inherited business interests, including Hughes Tool Company, a firm built by his father.[7]

Reagan, another example, was selected to participate in elected politics by a group of wealthy businessmen who needed a spokesperson for their conservative views. Another absentee leader, a university president, was pushed onto a board of trustees by powerful administrators for his willingness to merge two previously institutionally separate campuses—one a medical campus and one an academic campus—without interfering with the operation of either. Administrators on each campus knew that by encouraging the selection of an absentee leader, their own campus fiefdoms would be left largely autonomous and intact, with the overall structure largely a shell. In both instances the motives and policies of sponsors were unquestioned and were largely implemented.

How do absentee leaders get their leadership positions if they, by and large, are removed from the daily operations of the organization? What are they good at? Usually, absentee leaders are good at the symbolic trappings of leadership and maintaining consensual relations with followers. When ceremonies occur, absentee leaders look presidential or authoritative. Some are good, as was Reagan, in selected media formats. Others instinctively know or, more likely, have staff that know, the appropriate symbols to use that evoke the semblance of unity and harmony. Absentee leaders' own sense of inadequacy causes them to work very hard at convincing themselves as well as their followers that they are okay. In the process, they ignore problems, fluff over difficulties, and issue bland platitudes. In the short run, this convinces others that the organization is okay as well.

Indeed, absentee leaders seem to "play" at being leader rather than becoming emotionally or intellectually involved in the leadership process to the degree that trustworthy leaders would. It is no accident that one of the former careers of Reagan was being a B-grade Hollywood actor, and that others, such as Hughes, dabble in Hollywood, attracted by its tinsel. Actors are the intellectual cousins of absentee leaders. They share common characteristics, including considerable emotional detachment from their current activities, coupled with the ability to display the manifestations of emotion. Both "play" or perform their current roles, with scripts largely written by others, and do not actively engage in decision-making.

Likely Sources of Sense of Inadequacy for the Absentee Leader

Absentee leaders operate primarily at Maslow's level three. More than other transitional and toxic leaders, they desperately want to belong to the organizational group, even though they are unwilling or unable to meet the rigorous demands of true leadership. While street fighters want to be "king of the mountain," absentee leaders long to be "invited to the dance." When they are, usually by a group of powerful sponsors, they work to maintain the approval of their followers and sponsors, but secretly fear that someone someday will discover their social or professional inadequacy, and their invitations will be revoked. But rather than drive hard to learn the necessary skills to be a hit, they lurk in the shadows, hoping that no one will notice their lack of skills. When called on to perform publicly, they fall back on a set repertoire of tried and true skills and speeches that have worked successfully in other places and settings.

Absentee leaders never got beyond Maslow's level three in their own development, because they never developed the self-confidence to cease caring about being a part of the group as an end in itself, and to start caring about what one stands for when one joins the group. Ironically, some absentee leaders seem to exude confidence, but it is a charade for their publics, their employees, and their superiors. They follow a symbolic script on the job, frequently following rather than directing subordinates. The absentee leader's sense of inadequacy, usually present since childhood, causes a role reversal whereby staff and subordinates become the decision makers and the absentee leader tries to follow.

Absentee leaders typically developed their sense of inadequacy in childhood in response to factors beyond their control. But the sense of inadequacy for absentee leaders, unlike some types of toxic leaders, is a vague, dull ache that can be covered up and anesthetized by the pomp and circumstances and gay trappings of the symbolic aspect of leadership, as well as by play and leisure activities away from the job. These may be enough to prevent absentee leaders with underdeveloped morals from dwelling on and being depressed by their personal sense of inadequacy. Reagan, for example, did not dwell on the modest circumstances of his upbringing nor on his alcoholic father, escaping instead into Tinseltown and then the symbolic aspects of leadership. Hughes was bothered, for example, that while his exploits as a pilot, flying across the Arctic, in many ways surpassed those of Lindbergh, he did not receive the equivalent public acclaim, but dwelt more on other issues. By contrast, some toxic leader types become bitter, angry, and obsessed with their inadequacy to such a point that refuting and repressing it becomes a major preoccupation of life.

One of the childhood sources of inadequacy for absentee leaders may be a social background of lower middle class or less. Often raised by anxious, social-climbing parents unsure about their own social status and eager to have their children ascend the social ladder, such parents transmit their own sense of inadequacy to their offspring. Their children, including the prospective absentee leader, grow up vaguely aware that there is some social group of higher status to which they should aspire, and in which they could be happy if only they could belong. But once admitted to the social group, by dint of their usefulness in manipulating symbols and stating doctrines of the group, the absentee leader's sense of inadequacy abates only intermittently.

Further, most absentee leaders must worry about having the one thing that has gained them access—their leadership positions—taken away. This worry produces an indecisiveness uncharacteristic of most other transitional and toxic leader types. Absentee leaders also minimize time and effort at work, so as to minimize exposure that could bring about their removal from the leadership position that provides their access to desirable people and social circles.

Another source of feelings of personal inadequacy for absentee leaders is related to the first factor of being from a lower-middle-class or lower-class background. Some absentee leaders are offspring of recent immigrants, or aware that their families were immigrants in the not too distant past. Thus, absentee leaders are more likely than other transitional and toxic leaders to be from different ethnic and religious origins than the majority of the employees and managers where they work. Despite the American myth of the melting pot, these immigrant origins cause absentee leaders to have a sense of being different. Having struggled to move into the desirable group, once there, absentee leaders with different origins still feel like they do not belong. Their response to the internal cognitive dissonance is withdrawal through absenteeism. Samuel Pierce, the secretary of HUD in the Reagan administration when major scandals emerged in that department, was not only a minority (African-American), but one of the few high ranking African-Americans in an administration not known for equal opportunity, administering programs perceived to disproportionately benefit minorities. Such a position contributed to a sense of isolation and difference.

A third source of absentee leader feelings of personal inadequacy is a rigid, stern upbringing. Rather than confront the perpetrators, whether parents, relatives, or religious and educational figures, with challenges to the rigidness, absentee leaders pursue the path of least resistance and withdraw. Cleverly, they withdraw emotionally, placating stern authority figures on the surface, while secretly withdrawing and "not giving a damn" about their behavior, decisions, and consequences. This response is passive aggressive, and allows the absentee leader to refute earlier repressive authority figures subconsciously and covertly. The absentee university president, for example, used to recount how his parents made him perform home chores and school work to perfection, a duty he sometimes avoided by not coming home. This pattern of behavior carried over in later years to his interactions with trustees.

Yet a fourth source of inadequacy feelings that spans social classes and ethnic groups is mediocre talent. Absentee leaders are not known for their intellectual acuity and prowess. Conversely, leaders with considerable mental acuity and prowess usually like flexing it in the biggest possible arena. Absentee leaders frequently were mediocre students and mediocre performers in earlier careers and jobs until lifted to positions of higher leadership by either circumstances or powerful sponsors or some combination of both. Thus, absentee leaders remain unsure about their skills, like relying on an array of tried and true skills they know works for them, and avoid exposure in decision-making areas where their skills and information base will be challenged.

Reagan, for instance, was a B-grade movie actor before entering politics. His movie career had sputtered when he was offered the opportunity to become the spokesperson for General Electric, beginning a career as spokesperson for conservative causes. While his acting skills proved mediocre pitted against the competition in Hollywood, against sometimes lackluster and boring politicians, his presentation skills pushed him to the head of the pack.

ABSENTEE LEADERS AND THE ORGANIZATION

Operational Style and Tactics of the Absentee Leader

The most distinguishing operational style of absentee leaders is their assiduous avoidance of conflict and concurrent almost obsequious cultivation of consensus. Absentee leaders do not like conflict. They will avoid it at almost any cost, including removal of themselves from the organization emotionally, and if necessary, physically, by extensive traveling, long vacations and weekends, and short workdays and workweeks. Absentee leaders may not care who is making decisions, as long as whoever it is does not threaten their social standing and group belonging via threats to their leadership positions. Nor do absentee leaders care for subordinates who allow or generate conflict, for conflict punctures the peaceful, harmonious childhood created within the organization that absentee leaders craved when they were young.

When subordinates or opponents challenge the absentee leader's position, initially the absentee leader may seem indifferent, taking a long time to come to a decision to resolve the matter. But once decided, the absentee leader acts with startling quickness and even, rare for the absentee leader, brutality, banishing the threatening opponents from the organization, if possible, and dismissing them readily from mind. The absentee leader has fine-tuned the skill of dismissing from consciousness unpleasant memories since childhood. Hughes used to dismiss trusted employees with years of loyal service seemingly at a moment's notice (and usually through a proxy). Even the avuncular Reagan dismissed Donald Regan, former head of Merrill Lynch, secretary of the treasury, and then chief of staff, and Michael Deaver, trusted White House associate, with sudden swiftness when both became liabilities and allowed conflict (especially Regan) to fester.

The threatening employees, once dismissed organizationally or rendered ineffective and neutralized, are likewise dismissed from consciousness, as if they never existed. While brutal to the affected employees who have whole chunks of their working lives blocked out of consideration by their former leader, this behavior is less malicious than that of toxic leader types who attribute evil to opponents and, in some instances, set out to destroy opponents for no other reason than revenge.

Impact of the Absentee Leader on the Organization

The irony of absentee leaders is that the conflict they most wish to avoid eventually engulfs their organizations or key parts of it. Absentee leaders create a leadership and power vacuum. While they are out playing golf and jetting around, their vice presidents, deans, division heads, bishops, and other lower level leaders are lining up to do battle. Trustworthy leaders among these subordinates present proposals and visions, in the absence of any vision or substantial guidance from the absentee leader. Transitory and toxic leaders are threatened by these proposals, gear up to combat them, the trustworthy leaders, and each other. Infighting ensues. Sometimes substantial infighting does not occur until after a period of slow "leadership drift," not unlike continental drift, in which the organization languishes in the doldrums while other agencies and organizations with visionary leaders zoom ahead. Sometimes, however, the infighting breaks out immediately.

The organizations of absentee leaders come to resemble Europe or China during their feudal baron periods. There is no coherent whole, and overall policies are loose, at best. The quality of governance, decision making, and employee relations as well as productivity is very uneven, varying tremendously among subunits within the organization. Those subunits with solid, strong, trustworthy leaders are governed comparatively well and have relatively high productivity. Those subunits headed by transitory and toxic leaders are governed comparatively poorly and have relatively low productivity. Eventually, due to the power vacuum created by the absentee leader, the toxic leaders of subunits will make bids for ever greater amounts of organizational turf. Some will act increasingly arbitrary within their own units, being cautious at first, but then abandoning caution when they discover that the absentee leader does not seem to care what they do.

The quality of life in organizations headed by absentee leaders depends on the quality of subordinates. Yet absentee leaders do not devote enough time and attention to recruiting high quality people for major positions below them. They tend to accept whatever and whomever others below them suggest, failing to counter the self-serving motives that some subordinates may have in making personnel recommendations. Thus, the organizations headed by absentee leaders are inevitably neglected, and when economic conditions are harsh, these organizations drift into decline. When economic conditions are stable or favorable, these organizations stagger along with mediocre and uneven performances when they could be much better.

When the organization has a sizeable collection of toxic leaders heading subunits, destructive turf battles and self-aggrandizing behavior at the expense of the total organization ensues. Sensing opportunities under absentee leaders, this type of organization across a short time tends to attract a disproportionate share of toxic leaders to head or work in subunits or other key positions, and leadership drift turns into covert and overt warfare.

Protecting Yourself Against an Absentee Leader

What should you do if you find yourself working in an organization headed by an absentee leader, and you have no immediate opportunity for leaving the organization? How can you make the best of the situation in which you find yourself? Absentee-leader led organizations can degenerate into battle zones as subordinates fight for turf and power, but this process can be thrown into remission by a number of strategies. The best strategy for self-preservation is to create an organization that runs itself with as little intervention and assistance from the absentee leader as possible. In essence, coworkers and subordinates can work around the absentee leader's absences and delegate as much as possible.

Find others to conduct substantive leadership functions while the absentee leader carries out symbolic functions. If the absentee leader is a good manipulator of symbols and good at speaking, use the leader in that function. Encourage the absentee leader to expand on these attributes, gaining public visibility for the organization and projecting the desired image to key constituencies. Delegate other leadership functions to the extent possible to associates and trusted advisors.

Develop routinized decision structures to make evaluations and decisions, even when the absentee leader does not. A major weakness of the absentee leader is the absence of evaluation and decisions. Thus, routinize this process as much as possible, so that it occurs whether the leader is present or not. Set up regular schedules for plans, mission evaluations, and field reports. Have financial and budget meetings without the leader. Allow others to make operational and tactical decisions, consulting with the absentee leader only when major strategic issues are in question, and sometimes, not even then.

Try to transfer to a unit headed by a trustworthy leader. If infighting among subordinates has broken out or is about to break out, try to shift to a division that is headed by a trustworthy leader, not a toxic leader, preferably an internally powerful, well-insulated division. This will allow you to continue to pursue desirable objectives, while at least partially protected by a supportive division head. When the organization is splitting up into good guys and bad guys, jump to the good guy side. In a transitional leader led organization, at least some divisions and units will continue to be well managed. The more decentralized the organization, the more this is true. Find one, and if possible, join it.

Encourage trustworthy leaders heading divisions or subunits to unify in common objectives that enhance the organization's mission. If infighting is prolonged or particularly acerbic, encourage trustworthy leaders who care about production and productivity to unite in common interests. Facilitate deals and "log-rolling" or trades between trustworthy leaders when possible. An atmosphere of trust within the whole organization may not be possible, but such an atmosphere among trustworthy leaders who continue to care about employees, clients, and output may be possible.

Absentee leaders are not the ideal type of leader—indeed, they are far from it. But if you find yourself in an organization run by one, here is one small thought for comfort: almost every other type of transitory and toxic leadership is worse.

NOTES

1. Marcia Lynn Whicker, "Managing and Organizing the Reagan White House," in *The Reagan Presidency: An Incomplete Revolution?* ed. Dilys M. Hill, Raymond A. Moore, and Phil Williams (London: Macmillan, 1990), pp. 48–67.

2. Noah Dietrich and Bob Thomas, *Howard: The Amazing Mr. Hughes* (Greenwich, CT: Fawcett Publications, 1972).

3. Michael Drosnin, *Citizen Hughes* (New York: Holt, Rinehart, and Winston, 1985), pp. 453–455.

4. Lou Cannon, *President Reagan: The Role of a Lifetime* (New York: Simon and Schuster, 1991), pp. 56–57.

5. Robert Serling, *Howard Hughes' Airline: An Informal History of TWA* (New York: St. Martin's, 1983).

6. Cannon, p. 796.

7. Tony Thomas, *Howard Hughes in Hollywood* (Secaucus, NJ: Citadel, 1985), pp. 15–17.

7

The Busybody

Thumbnail Sketch of the Busybody (Coordinating Leadership Style): Energetic and constantly in motion, busybodies crave attention and affection, are sometimes fearful of alienating others, and specialize in manipulation of opinion and rumor mongering. These transitional leaders coordinate activities of followers by setting themselves up as the center of a communications network so that others must constantly turn to them to "tattle" on others. They often fail to make decisions that resolve conflicts among subordinates, assuring that the flow of complaints and information about conflicts and therefore attention received will be continuous.

HALLMARK CHARACTERISTICS OF THE BUSYBODY

A primary identifying characteristic of busybodies is their restless often unfocused energy. Busybodies may jump from one topic to another with an abundance of energy, sometimes leaving their subordinates fatigued and even bewildered. They are truly busy bodies in perpetual motion, scanning, roving, pressing, talking, traveling, planning, plotting, giving speeches, cajoling, joking, flattering, and working—always working. Busybodies verge on being workaholics, putting in long hours at the office, thriving on the thrill of running ever harder. Because of their energetic motion, busybodies may not be in or at the office at any point in time, but are likely to be working elsewhere on office business.

One busybody who clearly left his mark on the financial world of the 1980s was Michael Milken, head of the high yield bond department at Drexel Burnham. Milken has been credited with (or accused of) almost single-handedly creating the junk bond market.[1] Fascinated with the potential for low-grade bonds not rated by the major bond rating companies of Standard & Poor and Moody's since his college days at Berkeley and graduate school days at the University of Pennsylvania's Wharton School, he recognized there was no formal organized market for these securities.[2]

By dint of energy, insight, and constant work, Milken personally became the market for these securities, eventually dubbed "junk bonds" by the press and others. He initially pressed for expansion of their conventional use to fund capital expansions for medium- and small-sized companies, especially entrepreneurial efforts. But soon becoming bored with that, he began to pioneer junk bonds for leveraged buyouts in which the assets of the company involved became the collateral for the massive debt the managers incurred to take the company private, in many instances being stripped and sold. Even that use reached saturation, and then Milken, still in frenetic motion, brainstormed the use of junk bonds for hostile takeovers. Before being indicted on a series of charges, Milken was pushing junk bonds to the Japanese.[3] Eventually Milken became identified with and blamed for much of the high rolling financial excesses of the eighties.[4]

The Drexel high yield bond department reflected the urgency of a massive war or political campaign during Milken's leadership. After several years in New York, Milken moved the department to his native southern California, living in his home town of Encino and working in Los Angeles. In part he did this to remove members of the department from distractions in New York City, including drinking with members of other investment and trading houses at Wall Street watering holes after work. Members of the department had little time outside of work. Milken arrived at work each day at 4 A.M. to prepare for the opening of the financial markets in the east, which were three hours ahead. Other department members soon followed. Despite the early arrival, the work day would extend to 8 P.M. or longer for Milken. Working on Saturdays and Sundays was common. Milken kept two assistants busy just organizing and filing his work. When he traveled, he usually took along huge bags of company prospecti, always looking for the next trade and deal. While other colleagues hated long flights, Milken loved 12-hour flights overseas for the uninterrupted work time it provided him. Milken's prodigious income matched his prodigious efforts. Between 1983 and 1986, he earned over $550 million from trading and various deals and paid more income tax than any other U.S. taxpayer.[5]

Busybody Donald Trump exhibited similar compulsions toward work. Trump was constantly riding around Manhattan, Atlantic City, and other sites for his real estate ventures, looking for building locations, especially the preferred "Tiffany" location.[6] He visited construction sites regularly to inspect building progress on his mammoth projects: Trump Towers, Trump Plaza, Trump Castle, and others. Trump dispersed his energies broadly, eventually overseeing attractions in his Atlantic City properties, writing books, and negotiating with banks, investors, politicians, city officials, and others.[7] Unlike Milken who eschewed socializing and social events, except for those connected to his synagogue and charities, Trump frequently socialized on the New York scene, spilling over to parties and events in Aspen, Atlantic City, Southampton, and other places where the rich gather.[8] Trump was so involved with his work and so little involved with his family that he did not know the names of the schools his children attended. His secretaries kept track of their birthdays, shopped for his children, and got reports from the children's nanny to prompt Trump to ask about important events in their lives.

At times, former president George Bush exhibited the busybody characteristics of high energy levels and a lack of focus. He often seemed to have a personal perpetual motion machine driving him. His schedule was hectic and even frantic, but the lack of a specific agenda that had been a hallmark of the White House during the Reagan years made much of Bush's motion appear almost random. Bush traveled frequently abroad. By the end of 1990, halfway through his first and only term, Bush had visited twenty-nine countries, as many as Reagan visited during his two terms in office.[9] Berman and Jentleson describe Bush's style as one of "sheer personal energy."[10] Only the Persian Gulf War in 1991 curbed his travels abroad. Bush entertained frequently at both the White House and Camp David, giving the appearance of abhorring solitude.

Nor did Bush's characteristic of energetic motion diminish with his election defeat in 1992. During his lame duck period, Bush seemed to pick up the pace of actions in his favored sphere of foreign policy; for example, he resumed the bombing of Iraq. Even so, his advisors worried about his mental health and his seeming depression. They encouraged Bush to consider humanitarian intervention in Somalia. A major factor contributing to Bush's action, however, was his nervous energy as well as his advisors' concern for dispelling his post-election depression by renewed action. Throughout his administration, Bush's informal speaking style was uneven and irregular, indicating a difficulty to focus on a linear thought pattern from beginning to end. News magazines and papers regularly published "Bushisms" and "Bush-speak," examples of staggered, choppy sentences, when Bush spoke off-the-cuff.[11] Yet Bush spoke to the press more often than other modern presidents.[12]

This perpetual motion of busybodies undermines reflection, introspection, and intellectualism. On a daily basis, busybodies may seem decisive, as Milken did placing buy and sell orders, as Trump did cutting deals, and as Bush did during the Persian Gulf War. But busybodies do not excel at examining and questioning long-term strategies and goals. Once set in motion in a particular direction, they continue in that direction unchecked, until halted by external events rather than internal concerns. Thus, Milken never questioned the utility and uses of junk bonds, even when Securities and Exchange Commission investigations and charges from the U.S. attorney for securities violations loomed large. Trump was halted in his efforts to transform the New York City and Atlantic City skylines with ever bigger and more glorious buildings only by the collapse of the real estate market at the end of the 1980s and the concomitant collapse of his own debt-riddled empire. The amorphous direction of the Bush administration was not questioned by him or by officials in his administration until after the defeat of 1992.

A second hallmark characteristic is how busybodies structure relationships, placing themselves at the center of their work environment. They have a coordinating style, making themselves the focus of communications, yet they are driven to facilitate and encourage communications even when gossip rather than an organizational purpose is served. Busybodies create communication patterns resembling the hub and spoke flight patterns common among air carriers in the United States. Busybodies set themselves up to be the hub, or center, of the communications network. Their subordinates and coworkers form the spokes. Given their formal leadership position, considerable communication would flow through the offices and across the desks of busybodies anyway. But busybodies, by dint of their personality and style, manage to force much more than normal communications under their control, even when doing so is clearly not efficient nor in the best interest of the organization and those involved.

In this central communication role, Milken took hundreds of phone calls each day. Despite the fact that Drexel in New York was parallel to and not subordinate to Milken's California department, communications, ideas, and information often flowed from Milken to New York rather than reverse. People seeking capital and people with capital all beat a path to Milken's door with the intention of making money. Milken became the communications center for his immediate office, for much of his company (definitely for its high-profit activities), and for the informal junk bond market.

Trump forced details concerning all aspects of a deal or construction project to flow through him. He became intimately involved in details down to decorating touches that most builders left to others, including personally overseeing the building of the waterfall in Trump Towers. Trump encouraged a rivalry between his first wife, Ivana, who was placed in charge of Trump Castle in Atlantic City, and Steve Hyde, his supervisor for his gambling properties. Only the helicopter crash death of Hyde and two other top officials in the casino properties division, Mark Etess and Jon Benenav, ended the rivalry. Trump's many marital dalliances, including the highly publicized one with Marla Maples, also placed himself at the center of communications and attention.

At times, as Trump's personal life showed, the communications around and about busybodies can assume a tabloid air. If actors are the intellectual cousins of absentee leaders who "play" at being leader without becoming emotionally involved, and if perfectionists are the intellectual cousins of controllers, then gossips are the cousins of busybodies. Gossips collect information about the affairs, both public and private, of others and transmit that information to interested parties. So do busybodies. Busybodies sometimes appear to be megaphones, rebroadcasting and amplifying for a bigger audience information they have just received from an employee or subordinate. Thus, gossips and busybodies are similar in their involvement through information transmission. Although Milken did not in his plea bargain admit to insider trading, he was accused of using information about hostile takeovers to maximum financial advantage.

Yet unless they are newspaper columnists or television reporters, gossips have no motive beyond achieving a sense of identity with others by vicariously sharing in their experiences. Busybodies not only transmit information, but sometimes repackage that information to their own benefit, selectively omitting key information to shape subordinate opinions, affect decisions, and implement preferred positions. At times, busybodies exaggerate other information for the same ends. The hostile corporate takeovers Milken financed fomented and used such rumors. A form of corporate greenmail developed where rumors themselves became a club to extract payments from target companies, whether or not there was truth behind the rumors.

If there is no legitimate information, less benign busybodies will at times manufacture some, by passing forward information flimsily based in fact, and at times, in unfounded rumors. Busybodies are skilled at innuendo and at developing impressions among others as much as from what is implied in an emotionally charged environment as from what is said. Invariably, these rumors work on the surface to the benefit of maintaining the busybody's authority and power, and to implementing preferred positions. Once an unfounded rumor is loose, various subordinates react differently, and their reactions to the rumor or rumors become the basis for more information that the busybody can package, repackage, and manipulate to advantage. Frequently, the rumors circulated by busybodies have one group of subordinates pitted against another, for being relatively weak, busybodies retain control by a divide and conquer strategy.

Trump both used gossip about others when making deals and, eventually, thrived on being the source of gossip. At times, he would personally call reporters to spread rumors about himself, including rumors about his extramarital affairs. But the most clever use of rumors Trump employed was disseminating highly inflated and false figures about his net worth and assets to encourage banks and investment houses to continue to loan him ever larger sums of money. Trump planted rumors in the press that he was worth over $3 billion, not identifying that such estimates took unrealistically optimistic views of the value of real estate properties and failed to net out Trump's huge debt. Bush succumbed to rumors, innuendo, and negative advertisements in his presidential campaigns, particularly in his "Willie Horton" ad.

Further undercutting the leadership effectiveness of busybodies is the fact that all their internal information packaging and repackaging and outright rumormongering takes considerable time and energy. Busybodies may meet frequently with subordinates to create, quell, dispel, and disavow rumors circulating through the organization. Since much of this information manipulation has no organizational purpose beyond the perpetration of busybody power, productivity begins to suffer. In later stages of organizational decline, productivity is handicapped greatly, since rumor manipulation requires written memos as well as much time spent in meetings and massaging others.

Unlike some toxic leaders who appear to be sullen and angry most of the time, or who are unavailable and unapproachable, busybodies are both accessible and approachable. Busybodies are relatively charming and affable on the surface and appear to be good listeners. They generally strive to make interactions with them a pleasant experience so that people will continue to interact and provide the gossipy information that is the lifeblood of the busybody's organizational life. Thus, Milken rarely raised his voice and was regarded by his company associates as a truly nice guy. Trump would cruise and shmooze at his favorite upper east side watering holes in New York City and mingle with people at his various functions, events, and casinos. While he was prone to fits of vituperation against family members and close associates, he could definitely turn on the charm when he felt it was called for—with politicians, women he was pursuing, financiers, society people, potential business associates, and others. Bush was a "hale fellow well met" who, despite venal campaigns, was regarded most of the time as affable and reasonably approachable.

Busybodies usually have their door open. When lowly subordinates call to get appointments with comparatively high level busybodies, they are able to do so with comparative ease, since busybodies are afraid not to grant an audience to any supplicant. They never know, by such denial, what key information they will miss, who is fighting with whom, and indeed, whether or not malicious rumors are circulating about themselves. Thus busybodies seem to give lowly as well as highly placed employees equal time. This tendency sometimes produced cost overruns for Trump on construction projects. He would walk around a site and after receiving various advice from workmen at all levels, would then order expensive and needless changes to accommodate the concerns he heard.

Indeed, this tendency to give equal time to all who might come bearing gossip and rumor is part of another general characteristic busybodies exhibit—the failure to differentiate. In the world of rumormongering, all are equal as potential sources. And similarly, all are equal in the potential harm they might inflict by starting malicious rumors, and thus must be treated equally. Busybodies fail to distinguish between the more productive and less productive employees, and between those who contribute to the organization and those who are destructive toward its operation and even existence.

Likely Sources of Sense of Inadequacy for the Busybody

Busybodies fear being left out of the group. Outside of the group, the world is dark and lonely. Inside the group, the world is active, brightly lit, and vibrant. They are similar to small children who whistle because they are afraid of the dark. For such children, the noise, even though they personally are generating it, makes them think they are not alone in a dark night. For busybodies, the organizational din that results from communications, phone calls, lunches, cabals, and rumors flying, as well as the responses of victims and perpetrators, makes busybodies temporarily forget their fear of intellectual and emotional darkness outside of the organization and group. The greater the noise, the more busybodies are distracted from their fear.

For Trump, the group was the amorphous jet-set crowd that frequented posh places in New York, Aspen, Telluride, and beyond. Indeed, Trump bought a yacht, the Trump Princess, that was billed as the most elaborate and luxurious yacht ever built. It had a helipad, swimming pool, discotheque, screening room, minihospital, dining room with a gurgling waterfall, three elevators, gold-plated bathroom fixtures, and 250 telephone lines. The yacht was leased to Trump Castle for $400,000 per month, and to sail it to Atlantic City required Trump to pay $1 million to dredge the Absecon Channel to prevent the trophy ship from dragging bottom.[13] Yet Trump sailed on the ship only once and spent only one night on it. His organization, rather, used it for elaborate parties for society people and business associates, buying Trump entry into this group.

The group to which Milken, a more private person, belonged was much smaller, and possibly more powerful—the group of behind-the-scenes financiers that raised capital for some of America's biggest ventures during that decade, including Ted Turner's CNN. For Bush, the group was high level, well-heeled, and properly connected Republicans with similar backgrounds, such as those who belonged to his cherished Yale club of Skull and Bones.

Busybodies deeply want to belong to the group so they will not be afraid. In groups, they find meaning and a sense of importance. Outside groups, they find nothing. If they did not exist in a group, busybodies would be forced to create and perform work as an individual, and despite being workaholics, busybodies cannot function well as individuals. More than other types of transitional and toxic leaders, they can thrive only within the context of a communications network and through the efforts of others. Milken's astounding financial success depended deeply upon the decisions of others to invest, buy, sell, and conduct deals. Without this network, his commissions and energy had little meaning. Trump needed banks and other financiers for his deals, and then a small army of employees and workers to carry out his dreams of constructing ever larger buildings, all bearing his name. Bush was a creature of political organizations and bounced easily from one to another—from being ambassador to the United Nations to chairman of the Republican National Committee to chief U.S. liaison in China to director of the Central Intelligence Agency to vice president of the United States.[14]

Busybodies operate at Maslow's level three concerned with social belonging, but sometimes slide down to level two. Trump, in particular, would fall down to level two, attacking his family members and close associates, berating and belittling them in front of others. Associates reported episodes of Trump disparaging and even once raping his first wife, Ivana, belittling his mistress in public, and blaming his top organizational officials, dead from the helicopter crash, for business difficulties.[15]

Busybodies may appear to be innovative in some instances, but generally do not like or support change that fundamentally upsets the existing social order, except, perhaps, to enhance their own position within it. By becoming expert in rumors and gossip, busybodies use information as a control device to enable them to retain power. They also are soothed by the idea that nothing has changed, that people, especially subordinates, still fight and quarrel and spar as they always have. The conflict busybodies facilitate and at times generate has a soothing constancy to it and prevents more frightening substantive change. Indeed, busybodies will suffer verbal attack from others to keep feeding and receiving rumors.

Busybodies are particularly afraid of being excluded from the group. The sources of fear may vary from individual to individual and likely lie buried deeply in childhood. Despite their fear of being left out of the group and of radical changes in the social order (that may result in them being further left out), busybodies have a tremendous power of denial. Indeed, their fear drives the denial to the point of making them at times appear fearless, a paradox for busybodies.

Milken's father, for example, was crippled by childhood polio and grew up in an orphanage, yet Milken was able mentally to deny that his father limped and contended that he attended a boarding school.[16] Milken, who grew up on the "wrong" or north side of Ventura Boulevard in Encino, seemed incapable of registering this social fact despite being a near-genius in school and at other tasks, until years later, when he moved back and bought one of the most prized homes—Clark Gable's old estate—on the "right" or south side of the Boulevard.

Trump, as the second son and not his father's namesake, constantly challenged and fought with his father to gain his attention and affection, and to supersede his less talented and alcoholic brother. Trump so denied the problems his older brother had with drinking and finding his footing against a domineering father that he devoted only two pages to Freddie in his autobiography, and did not acknowledge that Freddie died from alcoholism at age forty-three. A troublesome child often playing pranks and creating mischief, he was sent off to the New York Military Academy to "straighten out," and there encountered students from a social background higher than his own. By then, his father, a builder of substantial but lesser success than son Donald would achieve, was in trouble himself, accused of pocketing illegal profits from contracts with the city to build moderate income housing. Trump was forced to downplay and deny these embarrassing family problems and to use his talents and charm to be included in a group that now was of higher social background than his previous school or neighborhood. Despite all his braggadocio and financial wherewithal, he never ventured in business far beyond the familiar turf of New York and New Jersey where he grew up.

Busybodies may be fearful of being targeted for administrative or legal attacks, although sometimes they even fear physical attack. One university administrator who was a busybody leader had been at several previous institutions and had been shot by his wife's ex-husband. In a fit of rage, the former husband, also an established professional with a Ph.D., had flown across the country, melodramatically stormed into this busybody's office brandishing a pistol, accused the busybody of stealing his wife, and then shot the busybody. The reaction of this university administrator was to move and then to deny the episode occurred. He never discussed this past trauma or admitted it to his subordinates in his new location, but rather ignored it, perhaps deceiving himself about how small the world is and how rumors know no institutional or geographic boundaries. Later, his new subordinates, learning about the trauma anyway, attributed much of his indecisiveness to being fearful, in part, because he had been shot. That he remained fearful was reflected by a poignant subsequent event. Once when working in an office with a small female subordinate on a weekend, noises of a possible intruder sent him scurrying into his office where he locked the door, leaving his considerably smaller female subordinate to fend for herself, which she did. Such were the actions of a man fearful of physical as well as other threats, traumatized by having been shot.

Other busybodies have been traumatized by similar threatening events. But other transitional and toxic leaders in similar settings would have responded differently, lashing out and viciously smashing threats. Busybodies, instead, seek the safety of crowds. That crowds and groups provide some protection from attacks and threats explains the habit of busybodies of needing groups and crowds, even conflicted ones. Thus, Milken continued his normal business and group activities even while legal attacks, investigations, charges, and subpoenas were accumulating. He hoped that by hiring the best lawyers, he could avoid the worst consequences of charges brought against him, and when presented with a plea bargain, initially seemed incapable of making a decision.

Many busybodies have been taunted and traumatized by bullies and other aggressive types in the past, and were too weak or too indecisive to defend themselves alone. Because busybodies are fearful generally, they want the protection of group membership even more than they want to bring their former attackers to justice, which is why they operate at Maslow's level three, but barely. They use a coordinating style to assure both their own membership in the group and that the organization functions to protect and comfort them.

When busybodies are feeling stronger, they may release their own hostile feelings through passive aggression, by creating rumors that pit one group against another. But busybodies rarely if ever make attacks directly, preferring to hide behind and in the group. Trump's father was particularly rough and hard on his sons, and years later Trump would repeat with pride many times how he learned to stand up to his father's dominance and bullying techniques. But many busybodies who were bullied seek solace and protection in the crowd, beginning a long-standing behavior. Even Trump sought the protection of his organization, which made him more powerful and able to defend himself against attacks and charges from others, including his father.

BUSYBODIES AND THE ORGANIZATION

Operational Style and Tactics of the Busybody

Because busybodies care more about group membership than about justice, they assume other employees feel similarly, when other employees may not. Others may feel enraged at injustices, and will challenge the busybody who does not deal with behaviors that bring about injustices, perceived or real. Thus, busybodies may overlook reports of petty graft by subordinates, of credential misrepresentation, and of raises and rewards not linked to productivity as largely irrelevant to their own role of mastering communications and rumor flow rather than making informed decisions. Yet others are unwilling to overlook these problems and pursue remedies that involve going around or over the head of the busybody in the organizational structure. Such pursuits create more conflict. Embedded in the busybody's own behavior, then, are the seeds of challenges and impetus for organizational decline.

Milken, for example, remained stunned at the furor the government and particularly the U.S. attorney's office in south Manhattan exerted to bring him down—millions of dollars and hundreds of thousands of manhours in investigations, plus giving prosecutorial immunity to others, such as Ivan Boevsky, who did trade on inside information, a charge never proved against Milken. Their outrage exceeded his offenses, he thought, and he was a scapegoat since he was prosecuted criminally for what had previously been viewed as technical violations subject to minor fines. Yet Milken did not understand that their outrage was not just at specific violations, but at his practices and the symbolism of his financial excesses.

Busybodies do not work at home, because busybodies construe their work as listening to petitions from plaintiff employees. Busybodies think they make tough decisions, but, in fact avoid confrontation and rarely buck majority opinion within the organization, for to do so might jeopardize the very group membership they so crave and need. Milken later concluded that his one problem was being too nice—financing too many deals and helping too many people, being unwilling to say no in a confrontational manner and turn down an eager client with some enthusiastic support in the Drexel organization.

Busybodies are almost never willing to use the full powers of their office to implement a controversial decision. When one busybody leader was asked by one plaintiff why he did not forcefully tell another employee that the employee was out of bounds, he responded that telling the employee his behavior was out of bounds would not change the behavior. This busybody, as is generally the case with this type of transitional leadership, failed to recognize the incentives at his command to effect both individual and organizational change. Indeed, busybodies are not concerned with organizational change or the organization generally except as it promotes their goal—financing deals for Milken, building property monuments for Trump, achieving higher and higher political offices with few visions of what to do with them for George Bush. But since busybodies generally are afraid of change, preferring petty conflict among subordinates to change, failure to use leadership powers to cause change is unsurprising.

Despite all their apparent openness, busybodies often do not develop a walk around style of management where they walk around the organization unannounced, to give shy, busy, or otherwise involved employees a chance to reach them, and to observe first-hand what is going on. Trump was an exception to this tendency, and even his "walking around" was episodic rather than consistent, with him neglecting some properties for considerable time periods.

What is going on in the organization in terms of actual work is more boring to the busybody than the information, gossip about personal peccadillos and worse, and rumors and reports on sometimes raging factional battles that naturally stream through his door if he just stays in his office and encourages such flows. Busybodies may lose touch with what is actually going on in the organization. Milken remained surprised at who crossed over and testified for the government within his own organization.

Impact of the Busybody on the Organization

Many busybodies have never been interested enough in the substance of the work of their organizations to acquire substantive skills. Later their own schedules of holding court over complaining employees prevents them from having the time to keep up with professional developments in the field to the same extent that trustworthy leaders or even other types of transitional leaders, such as the controller, would. Busybodies consequently often lack the technical skills to evaluate fully new product proposals and other proposed innovations, as well as the emotional fortitude to risk embracing new ideas even if the outcomes of such evaluations were favorable. Busybody-led organizations are colorful places where everyone seems, well, busy feeding communication channels often with irrelevant or destructive information. But the longer they are led by a busybody, the less productive they become.

Milken obviously had substantial technical skills in junk bonds and kept up with financial fluctuations, but did not concern himself with the larger impact of the deals he financed on laid-off workers and disrupted and disemboweled companies. As the furor to junk bond finance began to feed on itself, some of the deals were not even financially sound in the long run, with companies acquiring such huge amounts of debt at such high interest rates that bankruptcy was inevitable. Ultimately, this lack of concern and junk bond financing fever turned back on Drexel and brought about its own bankruptcy. Trump's organization itself often did not know Trump's net worth, and was usually cash poor, with most of the assets being tied up in real estate. His subordinates were constantly shifting funds around to cover payments, and frequently launched into new projects without conducting prior cash flow analyses. Bush's decision to enter the Persian Gulf War with air strikes was made almost haphazardly and surprised even his own chairman of the Joint Chiefs of Staff, General Colin Powell.

Much of the information that streams to busybodies is bad. Satisfied happy employees do not rush off daily to tell the busybody leader how happy and satisfied they are. Rather, malcontents and complainers rush off to petition for personally favorable changes. Yet as time passes and productivity is lowered, even those employees that are happy will be less so. As the malcontents figure out how pliant and indecisive the busybody truly is, the factional infighting and conflict increases. Factions know the busybody will not punish other competing factions for misbehavior or inflicted injustices, and similarly they know that the busybody will not punish them. In fact, unlike the street fighter, the busybody does not traffic in rewards and punishments, regardless of merit or damage. The busybody traffics in information, good, bad, and malicious.

The organization headed by a busybody soon becomes a free-for-all. Like the absentee leader, the busybody, despite all the energetic motion and communication, creates a power vacuum that allows malcontents and other toxic leaders to perform as they like, and eventually attracts them. The power vacuum created by the absentee leader is from detachment and distance. The power vacuum created by the busybody is from distraction and indecisiveness. If the conflict that results in the absentee leader's organization is like an institutional conflagration, then the conflict in a busybody's organization is like an institutional hothouse fire fueled by a backdraft. Nobody benefits from the conflict in the long run, for it rapidly becomes destructive, with no strong leadership to counter personally aggrandizing employees and subordinate toxic leaders. Once again, productivity plummets. Despite the atmosphere of constant busy-ness, the activities of subordinates are increasingly devoted to covering and kicking asses, and everybody loses.

Protecting Yourself Against a Busybody

At least initially, busybody-led organizations can be fun places to work, since everyone is networking, coffee klatching, and doing lunch much of the time. You may get a sense of connectedness and belonging, at least until some of the more negative aspects of this type of organization become apparent. When and as they do, keep these strategies in mind:

Be as inconspicuous as possible. Busybody organizations feed on rumors and innuendo. Often facts are placed out of context, misquoted, and misrepresented. In this context, being inconspicuous is a good strategy—no attention is good; attention leads to likely distortion.

Realize that the organizational grapevine can strangle you. Even if the attention and focus you get in a rumor fed organization is positive in the short run, rumors can run amuck and eventually do you much harm. The organizational grapevine on which you swing through the corporate jungle today can be used to strangle you and hang you tomorrow. Unlike controller organizations where informal networks are often crucial to control the worst impulses of the controller, the busybody leader uses informal networks and their communications channels to control you. Do not get too wrapped up in these gossipy networks, for they detract from maintaining productivity, your only true defense against a rumor fed attack.

Watch your back. Intra-organizational conflict in some organizations is like warfare, with strategies and teams forming. In busybody-led organizations, if conflict erupts, it is more similar to guerrilla sniper fire, unexpected, with the origin not always clear, and frequently aimed at your back. At Drexel, for example, no one eventually was above suspicion for cooperating with the feds, and conversations often occurred in restrooms and kitchens with water running from faucets to make spoken words unintelligible to any listening devices.

Find an organizational haven. In some organizations, being sent to outer posts and hinterlands is bad for your career, keeping you away from the action. But in busybody-led organizations, isolation—both hierarchically and geographically—can provide a haven to protect you from the rumor mill and waste of productive time.

Know that the busybody, when challenged, will rarely fight. Finally, most busybodies want to avoid conflict and abhor any overt clashing that percolates up from below the surface. If you determine that your busybody leader fits this norm, in desperate situations you can challenge the busybody directly. The busybody will often back down to avoid a fight. Busybodies like little rumor fed conflicts below the surface where they can control and dominate the outcome. A knock-down-drag-out fight is not their format for conducting business. Milken, for example, ultimately decided to accept a government plea bargain rather than to fight through a drawn out emotionally draining trial. Trump, for another example, avoided expensive bidding wars with real estate rivals, often folding when threatened with competition for the same property. But he did not forget, and often came back another day when circumstances had changed to get his way.

NOTES

1. Connie Bruck, *The Predators' Ball: The Junk-Bond Raiders and the Man Who Staked Them* (New York: Simon and Schuster, 1988), pp. 10–20.

2. Jesse Kornbluth, *Highly Confident: The Crime and Punishment of Michael Milken* (New York: William Morrow, 1992), pp. 31–67.

3. Dan G. Stone, *April Fools: An Insider's Account of the Rise and Collapse of Drexel Burnham* (New York: Donald I. Fine, 1990), p. 43.

4. Benjamin J. Stein, *A License to Steal: The Untold Story of Michael Milken and the Conspiracy to Bilk the Nation* (New York: Simon and Schuster, 1992), pp. 15–27.

5. Kornbluth, p. 239.

6. Jerome Tuccile, *Trump: The Saga of America's Most Powerful Real Estate Baron* (New York: Donald I. Fine, 1985).

7. Trump wrote two books casting himself in a positive light and, according to others, especially Harry Hurt, containing exaggerations and lies. The first of these books is by Donald J. Trump with Tony Schwartz, *Trump: The Art of the Deal* (New York: Random House, 1987). The second was with Charles Leerhsen, *Trump: Surviving at the Top* (New York: Random House, 1990).

8. Harry Hurt III, *Lost Tycoon: The Many Lives of Donald J. Trump* (New York: W. W. Norton, 1993).

9. Larry Berman and Bruce W. Jentleson, "Bush and the Post–Cold War World: New Challenges for American Leadership," in *The Bush Presidency: First Appraisals*, eds. Colin Campbell and Bert A. Rockman (Chatham, NJ: Chatham House, 1991), pp. 93–128.

10. Ibid., p. 99.

11. Michael R. Beschloss and Strobe Talbott, *At the Highest Levels: The Inside Story of the End of the Cold War* (Boston: Little, Brown, 1993), p. 260.

12. Mary E. Stuckey and Frederick J. Antczak, "Governance as Political Theater: George Bush and the MTV Presidency," in *Leadership and the Bush Presidency: Prudence or Drift in an Era of Change?* eds. Ryan J. Barilleaux and Mary E. Stuckey (Westport, CT: Praeger, 1992), pp. 24–36.

13. Hurt, pp. 227–228.

14. William A. DeGregorio, *The Complete Book of U.S. Presidents*, 3rd ed. (New York: Wings Books, 1991), pp. 674–676.

15. See Hurt for numerous episodes scattered throughout the book.

16. Kornbluth, p. 33.

8

The Controller

Thumbnail Sketch of the Controller (Command Leadership Style): Rigid transitional leaders, controllers are traditionalists and perfectionists. Their need to command others leads them to micromanage organizational affairs. Unlike street fighters, controllers lack the charisma to attract huge crowds and followings. Controllers manipulate followers predominantly through the control and miscontrol of information. They control by elaborate and selective use of bureaucratic rules restricting and directing information to command the attention and obedience of followers.

HALLMARK CHARACTERISTICS OF THE CONTROLLER

Like the absentee leader and the busybody, the controller as a transitional leader is usually more benign and less malicious than toxic leaders—enforcers, street fighters, and bullies. But the controller is not quite as benign as the absentee leader. Controllers are more active than absentee leaders, and, with a command leadership style, have greater power needs. The hallmark characteristic of the controller is the need to be involved in almost all aspects of decision making. Controllers crave certainty and surety. The only way controllers feel they can achieve the certainty and surety they need is to make decisions themselves. This need, rather than any great vision of where the organization should go, or any special talent, is the reason controllers feel they must be involved.

Related to the need to be involved in most or all aspects of decision making is an inability to delegate. In contrast to absentee leaders who are willing to delegate almost everything as long as they still retain their own leadership posts, controllers do not delegate easily, readily, or sometimes at all, even when the organization would be better off if they did. Rather, controllers hold their organizational cards close to the vest, failing to involve others.

One well-known controller who has left a firm imprint on both the private and public sectors is H. Ross Perot. Perot's energy and extensive schedule of appointments caused one news magazine to depict him as the energizer bunny, a pop culture icon used in advertising and known for its capacity to keep on going and going and going.[1] A billionaire by age thirty-eight, Perot's power came from his great wealth, which he attributed to luck.[2] Yet close associates credit his extraordinary energy and shrewdness, which he used to maintain tight command and control of the organizations he built. This characteristic was first exhibited in his actions at Electronic Data Systems (EDS), the company that brought his initial wealth, and continued through- out his aborted presidential campaign in 1992. Perot clung rigidly to a "Norman Rockwell" view of how the world and especially his organizations should be run, even hanging original Rockwell paintings in his Dallas office. To assure this view, he exerted command by involving himself in all aspects of decision making.

Another controller was William Casey, who held many positions in government, ranging from chief of the OSS in the European theater of operations in World War II to director of the Central Intelligence Agency in the Reagan administration.[3] Even before World War II, Casey was develop- ing rigid anti-communist views that made him the quintessential Cold War warrior, unbending in this view until his death. Critics contend that Casey's rigid adherence to this view led him to be involved with daily operations during his tenure as CIA director, including some illegal ones, such as the Iran-Contra affair.[4] Even before Reagan was elected in 1980, Casey was suspected of involvement with the October Surprise, an effort to delay the release of American hostages being negotiated by President Carter until after the 1980 election.[5] During his government service in the Reagan years, Casey's need to maintain personal control of his affairs caused him to eschew the normal practice of high level officials of placing their financial assets in a blind trust to prevent conflict of interest, and to keep control of his own stocks.[6]

At times, former president Jimmy Carter exhibited controller charac- teristics. He was a leader who thought deeply about governmental processes, procedures, and practices, expecting others to have the same fascination for such ordinarily dry topics as he himself did. His background in the U.S. Navy contributed to his command style leadership. He approached government from a military and engineering background, both of which provided ample training in the importance of rules, regulations, and laws. He funneled much information in his White House through himself, refusing initially to appoint a chief of staff to relieve some of the pressure on himself. His reluctance to delegate was legendary, including his personally scheduling matches on the White House tennis court. He attempted to reform government and gain control of the federal bureaucracy by introducing zero-based budgeting. Yet he was not skilled with working with congress, and as an outsider in Washington, never cultivated key contacts needed to function effectively. Most observers feel that his obsession with details and perfection contributed to his defeat in 1980.

Controllers do not delegate and try to remain involved in all aspects of decision making for a variety of reasons. One is that they are perfectionists of a sort, and fear that others will not make the correct decisions, where "correct" is defined as the same decision the controller would have made under identical or merely similar circumstances. Perot, for example, wanted his employees and recruiters to present a certain image—one reflecting conservative and even militaristic values. Not trusting his workers to select their own wardrobes, he created a company dress code that dictated dark suits, white shirts, narrow ties, and shined shoes. When the recruiters descended upon San Francisco, *San Francisco Chronicle* columnist Herb Caen discussed it unflatteringly in a column titled "Space Age Company Has Stone Age Dress Code."[7] Dozens of employees clipped the column and mailed it anonymously to company officials, but the dress policy did not change.

Wanting to be involved in all aspects of policy development, Carter initially refused to appoint a White House chief of staff. He served as his own chief of staff, until overwhelmed, he was forced to recognize the need for an assistant whose primary function was to screen appointments and shield the president from information and attention-demand overloads. Only in 1979 did Hamilton Jordan officially assume this role after Carter's election in 1976.

A second reason controllers do not delegate is that they abhor disorder, and delegation necessarily involves a certain amount of disorder and slippage in the lines of communication across different people. This slippage is especially true when an organization is populated with employees from diverse backgrounds. Perot tried to avoid this disorder for EDS by recruiting only married white men with a military background and at least five years of work experience.[8] Yet he demanded eighty-hour work weeks from them for "niggardly" salaries, and work often involved substantial travel.

The recruiters for Perot's company especially had a brutal schedule, making for a difficult home life. Recruiters would fly out to a distant location and interview EDS job applicants from morning to night for ten straight days, from Monday of one week through Wednesday of the next week. Only one out of seventy of the job interviewees would survive the recruiting process of written tests, spouse interviews, team interviews, and final appraisals by an officer. Then the recruiters would fly back to Dallas to catch up on paperwork on Thursday and Friday. They would take Saturday off and fly out to a new location on Sunday to begin the process all over on Monday. Family difficulties ensued, as the recruiters on their one day off wanted a home-cooked meal, solitude and rest, whereas their lonely wives wanted a night out and conversation.[9] One solution considered was to hire single men, but Perot was wary of this, fearful that single men would not have the same commit-ment and would not be as focused on work.

A third and major reason that controllers do not delegate is that they need to command and fear losing control. This motive explains Perot's split with General Motors after EDS merged with GM. Perot had thought that EDS could be transferred into GM intact, so that GM managers could benefit from the can-do spirit of EDS executives. But the merger was a bad marriage. Perot did not exert the influence he felt he would and should, especially in changing GM's practices. Roger Smith, CEO at GM, proved to be a more formidable force than Perot anticipated. Misunderstanding compounded misunderstanding between the giant GM and Perot. Perot resisted a plan by GM to buy Hughes Aircraft and the handling of Class E stock.[10]

Perot had thought that he could sell EDS to GM and retain control, but had in fact lost control and, increasingly, patience. Relationships between Perot and GM deteriorated until GM paid $700 million to Perot to remove him and his meddling from the corporate giant. Perot lost control totally of EDS and gave a parting shot to GM in a closing press conference, announcing that GM was closing eleven plants, putting thirty thousand people out of work, cutting back on capital expenditures, losing market share, and having problems with profitability, even as it was signing an agreement to pay him $700 million to get rid of him. He, Perot, offered in a public bow to GM to give them a chance to come to reason and rescind their decision, an offer GM chose to decline.[11]

Controllers may lack an overarching vision of where the organization should go and how it should get there, but they do have strong preferences about how operations should be conducted. Controllers generally prefer neat, orderly processes. They use their leadership positions and power to bring about these processes. Persons who aid and abet them in this endeavor are regarded as friends and supporters. Persons who ask why any particular neat, orderly process is necessary and if it really contributes to the organizational mission are regarded as opponents not to be trusted.

Carter was criticized at times for letting the nation drift with an overloaded agenda and no clear sense of where the nation should be headed. Yet he had a clear sense of a need to restore a popular touch to government, eschewing the symbolic trappings of the presidency in favor of sweaters for fire-side chats, walking during his inaugural parade, and being called "Jimmy." While Carter's presidency did produce some significant achievements, especially the Middle East settlement between Anwar Sadat of Egypt and Menachem Begin of Israel, the deteriorating economy and lack of clear priorities from trying to do everything at once caused his administration to be plagued with a sense of drift throughout its duration.

Perot's clear sense of mission dissipated when he moved from the profit oriented world of business to the messier world of national politics. He correctly sensed that the national mood was one of increasing populist individualism, including a rejection of both mainstream political parties. Yet he offered up no clear vision of where the nation should be going, beyond pithy statements and criticisms of other plans. These pithy aphorisms worked well initially in the evolving world of talk show politics but ultimately failed Perot on the campaign trail.

Nor did Bill Casey's anticommunist beliefs translate into a specific vision of a world showing the first thaws of the Cold War and poised for communist collapse. As a consequence, he supported operational plans a clearer vision might have preempted.

Partly to compensate for their own sense of inadequacy, controllers seem to be, and at times are, disdainful of people who are not excited by or involved in the implementation of "efficiency incurring" processes to make everything neatly identified and hierarchical. Controllers often regard such people as not understanding and hopeless. Rather than try to deal with, educate, or otherwise bring questioning employees to their own point of view, controllers lose interest and move on to the next challenge. Controllers are committed to the organization, then, only if their own leadership positions remain intact.

Consider Perot's willingness to cut and run at GM when he found greater resistance to the corporate giant assuming the EDS philosophy than he anticipated. He began to regard GM executives as hopelessly resistant to changing more efficient methods that he knew and advocated, and incapable of reform. He exhibited somewhat the same attitude during his on-again, off-again then on-again presidential campaign in 1992. First, he declared the political process corrupt and mainstream politicians from both parties inca-pable of change. Then, he declared them reformed in July of 1992 when he withdrew. Months later, he declared them not reformed and the system needful of his leadership. His ambivalence reflected an underlying disdain that his notions and ideas were not more eagerly embraced on a broad scale, and a reluctance to educate over a period of years.

Controllers are sometimes described as perfectionists, but this term is slightly inaccurate, although both controllers and perfectionists have considerable overlap, especially in attention to details of a project. Like controllers, perfectionists devote considerable time and attention to details and to making sure the details are correct. Also like controllers, perfectionists are driven by a sense of inadequacy, but perfectionists are most fearful of rejection and criticism by others. Thus, perfectionists delay and procrastinate in completing tasks, ostensibly because more work is always needed to make the thing "right." The real reason for their delay, however, is to avoid criticism. As long as a project is never completed, it can never be realistically criticized, for it is still "in progress."

Controllers, by contrast, are fearful of rejection and loss of control. They devote time and attention to different details than do perfectionists. Controllers pay particular attention to the details of bureaucratic rules and regulations, for adherence to those details is important to their own capacity to command and to the maintenance of their own power and control. Perot's attention to the details of election laws in the fifty states was phenomenal, an attention that allowed him to circumvent normal party nomination processes and to get on the ballot by petition. Controllers may also pay considerable attention to the work details of any particular project, but usually to the form and style of the project as much as to its substance. This is because controllers perceive form and style to be crucial to the overall appearance of work output, and therefore to the approval it will receive from key decision makers. Approval is necessary for their retention of control. Perot's company dress code illustrates this point.

Because of their different underlying motives, controllers differ from perfectionists in their attitudes toward project completion. Perfectionists never want to complete projects, for doing so invites the criticism they abhor and find emotionally painful. Thus extreme perfectionists often have a stream of incomplete projects with few successes. Consequently, extreme perfectionists rarely become organizational leaders of any consequence. Controllers, however, have less difficulty in completing a project, once they are satisfied that sufficient attention to detail has been devoted and that their own positions of authority and leadership and platform from which they command will not be jeopardized. Indeed, controllers want to complete projects so that a string of timely successes will be credited to them. Controllers want the projects to be completed, however, in the "right" way. Perot, Carter, and Casey all achieved a considerable string of successes by the timely completion of many projects and tasks early in their careers.

An additional major characteristic of controllers is their considerable rigidity in their approach to work, indeed, to life, and their need to command subordinates to do things their way. Often tasks must be accomplished their way or not at all. Their normal attentiveness to bureaucratic rules and regulations can become obsessive at times. They are sufficiently well versed in organizational rules as to use them as weapons against others if and when they are challenged or attacked. Unlike bullies, however, who raise the use of organizational rules as weapons to a warfare art form, controllers largely see the rules and regulations as necessary procedures to assure a smooth and steady outflow of work product, aware that a smooth and steady outflow of work product is necessary to assure their own control of leadership.

Likely Sources of Sense of Inadequacy for the Controller

Controllers can be small-minded and petty, and with some frequency are. They, like their more benign brethren, absentee leaders, operate at Maslow's level three—more concerned about social belonging and group participation than about safety from attacks. Controllers will fend off attacks from others within and without the organization as ferociously as any toxic leader. But their primary daily focus is not upon a level two us-versus-them, or even more paranoid, me-versus-them, mentality. Rather, their primary focus is upon achieving an efficient and effective organization to which they can belong and in which their own command of leadership is not questioned or challenged.

As with all transitional and toxic leaders, controllers are deeply insecure with a strong sense of personal inadequacy. But unlike absentee leaders, controllers are not concerned about social or class background, or other such "superficial" and "superfluous" phenomenon. Perot and Carter took pride in being from good, honest families where hard work was valued.

Nor are controllers insecure about their own technical knowledge and skills, for they work very hard, do their homework, and put in long hours. Perot drove himself as hard as his employees. Carter was legendary for long hours and thick briefing books. Both Perot and Carter attended the Naval Academy where discipline, subject mastery, and technical skills were stressed. A gifted student, Casey not only worked hard at his studies and later at writing and publishing, but also at athletics where he was not particularly talented.

Rather, the source of the sense of personal inadequacy controllers hold results from the fact that they are comparatively socially inept. This ineptness is not the result of class and background, but from personal insensitivity to the feelings of others. The command style of controllers, where they must have their own way at almost any cost, contributes to their social insensitivity. Controllers are not as skilled as are other transitional and toxic leaders at reading social cues. Frequently, they miss or misread social cues that others see and interpret accurately.

As children, controllers were the most likely to be called nerds and eggheads by playmates and schoolmates. Casey, for example, was shy as a youth, not particularly skilled with the girls, and a scholar who lacked the athletic skills of his younger brother. Perot's slight physical stature, big ears, and squeaky voice made him seem unremarkable in his hometown of Texarkana, where the fastest route to adolescent male glory was on the local football team. The quintessential Boy Scout, Perot appeared "square," eschewing drinking, dating extensively, and fast living. Even as adults, while other toxic leaders are focusing on the dynamics of group interactions and the personal reactions of others to their own leadership initiatives and behaviors, controllers are focusing upon technical details and bureaucratic rules. Carter, when running for president, ineptly declared he had lust in his heart, an inappropriate remark for the campaign, and one that baffled much of the public that regularly experienced lust and felt no need to declare it.

Having been excluded from groups in the past, or left behind without being included before they were even aware there was a group, controllers desperately want to belong. At a subconscious level, they remember that in the past, when others made the decisions and orchestrated group activities, they were left with no one to command and nothing to control. As adults, the only way they can be assured of being included is to make all the decisions themselves—thus their need to be involved in all aspects of decision making.

Further exacerbating their tendency to be over-involved in decision making and their failure to appropriately delegate authority is their recognition that they must rely more heavily upon technical skills and successful output, than other more winsome toxic leaders who can get by on charm, charisma, and braggadocio with little to back it up. Perot's petition drive to get on the presidential ballot resembled a romance with the public where he demanded signs of affection to perform—declaring he must have a requisite number of signatures in ALL fifty states, an unprecedented sign of affection, if he were to run.

Both absentee leaders and controllers are socially insecure, but the focus of the insecurity is different. Absentee leaders are more likely to be insecure about the social upbringing and type of family or religious and ethnic group in which they were raised. Sensing that this can never be changed by personal action, absentee leaders just withdraw. It is characteristic of the insensitivity that generally marks controllers that they dismiss the concerns of absentee leaders as irrelevant, failing to recognize how much such things matter to some people some of the time.

Controllers have learned through bitter experiences in the past that they are socially inept at a more personal level, and they strive to compensate by emphasizing the details of project or policy management at which they are good. Further, they feel that even if they are not as loveable as other types, the rules will protect them, hence, their great emphasis on and frequent over-reliance on organizational rules. The rule that Perot ultimately wielded with great force was the universally recognized golden rule of wealth: he who has the gold rules.

CONTROLLERS AND THE ORGANIZATION

Operational Style and Tactics of the Controller

Controllers force all or almost all aspects of organizational management to come through them for formal approval and sign-off. They spend time scrutinizing travel vouchers, grant and project expenditures, and the details of subunit budgets, rather than let auditors and subunit leaders have final approval. They also spend time reading and editing much of the formal correspondence that flows out of their division or organization, rather than delegate this responsibility to editors and project managers. One controller heading up a university research unit refused to allow routine letters to be sent from his unit before he read and approved each piece of correspondence first.

As a result of their involvement in even the smallest aspect of operations and refusal to delegate final approval of such details to others, controllers sooner or later (usually sooner) begin to feel tired and overwhelmed. As they become more and more exhausted, they become more irritable with the small rule violations that normally would not bother them. The more irritable they become, the more others shy away from them, thereby feeding at an unconscious and sometimes a conscious level the controller's insecurities about being socially inept.

Confronted with increasing work and decreasing time to deal with any single issue, controllers increase their own hours at work to try to meet all the demands they have placed on their own time, but even this is not enough. They may begin to demand that others increase their time at work also until, in extreme situations, the workplace resembles on the surface a haven for puritanical, rule-obsessed workaholics. But this semblance is only on the surface. Underneath, subordinates and employees become more and more angry at the inadequacy-driven irrationalities of the controller.

Eventually, talented people figure out that they have no control over their own work, since the controller has assumed final control of everyone's work for himself. Employees and subordinates will tolerate this up to a point, but eventually blowups between the controller and subordinates begin to occur. The more talented subordinates leave the organization or move to another part of it if transfers are an option. Carter, for example, was one of the few incumbent presidents in history to experience a challenge for renomination from within his own party, mostly from dissidents who felt they had been excluded by his control from involvement in setting and passing the national agenda, and who were convinced his leadership was ineffective.

Impact of the Controller on the Organization

One of the greatest impacts of having a controller-run organization is a noticeable lack of splendid talent in it. Talented and especially skilled employees get disgusted when they have little or no say in the final shape their products and projects assume and leave when more attractive options present themselves. Since people with talent and skills are more likely to be offered alternatives, and those with less talent and skills have fewer options, the latter begin to accumulate disproportionately in the organization. A major criticism of Carter, for example, was that he never expanded his circle of intimate advisors beyond his long-term supporters who were mostly from Georgia. His White House lacked those more talented with the environment of power politics in Washington and was deprived of diverse perspectives. Perot soon clashed with his top political advisors in his presidential campaign, because he refused to run ads they contracted, monitored every detail, and consequently caused advisors to leave shortly after joining the campaign.

Nor are talented employees who leave replaced with equally talented recruits. As difficulties with employees crop up, implying difficulties with the controller's commanding leadership, controllers become more threatened by others who will challenge their control. Controllers generally do not see an us-versus-them scenario in every issue, but in part, this is because they have controlled or eventually seized control of the employee hiring and selection process to make sure that no competition for their position is lurking a level or two down within the organization.

As organizational drift into decline begins, challenges to their own leadership and therefore avenue for assuring belonging to the group grow eminent. Controllers become even more reluctant to hire subordinates equally or more talented than themselves. An old dictum states that Grade A people hire Grade A people, while Grade B people hire Grade C people. Grade B people hire even less talented people than themselves so they do not risk having their own mediocrity in key skills exposed, causing themselves to be replaced. This dictum must have been written initially about a controller.

Controllers rarely have someone in training to replace themselves. In the event that a controller is suddenly removed or rendered unable to continue at work, often it takes two people to replace him. Controllers are comforted by this fact, and allude to how difficult it has been to find anyone to fill their shoes. Yet what this demonstrates, as much as anything, is the failure of the controller to cultivate the talent of others by training a replacement or others who might understand the nature of their own jobs. Controllers do not want to train replacements, even when it makes sound organizational sense to do so. If there is a replacement readily available, controllers fear that in due course, they will be replaced.

Controller-led organizations are also marked by a lack of innovation. In part, the dearth of innovation is because the most talented and innovative employees leave, but also because it is the controller's own rigidity, insistence on doing things his way, and overemphasis on rules and regulations that stifles innovation. One of the ways controllers assure their own position is to divide up tasks, so that no one person other than themselves has the big picture of projects and policies. Controllers justify this division as efficient functional specialization. But it also assures that no one will have the necessary information needed to replace the controller.

An unintended consequence of the above functional specialization and division of work is that no one else has the necessary vantage point to see how all the pieces fit together and therefore to make innovative suggestions. The organizational loss from the absence of innovative suggestions is less than it may seem, since controllers would likely ignore such proposals even if they were put forth. Controllers are big on receiving credit, personally, and suggestions put forth by others are often brushed aside. Such suggestions may appear later in slightly different form now put forth by the controller, who has convinced himself that he actually had the ideas first. Casey, for example, felt that his father worked hard, but did not get rewards for his work, something Casey avowed he would avoid. He argued that if your light is not shining from under a bushel, then remove the bushel and get credit for what you do, a philosophy he himself practiced with great success.

Protecting Yourself Against a Controller

Most controllers are not as extreme (nor as successful) as Perot. For a period, working for a controller-led organization can be exhilarating and exciting. Controllers give employees a sense of belonging to an efficient and well-run organization and, at least in the short run, a sense of mission. Eventually, however, the short-run goals do not appear to link to a long-run plan, and the controller's rigidity becomes tiring. The long hours at work with little relief may become exhausting, and the personal toll on families and relationships excessive. In some instances, controllers use the organizations' rules to promote their own personal idiosyncrasies. They may be impatient,

irritable, and irascibile. Perot, especially, was known to exhibit these characteristics toward employees, stirring up resentments as well as pride at belonging to an elite company.

What can you do if you find yourself working for a controller? Here are
some strategies:

*Try to establish limits on your organizational commitment, so that some areas
of your life are personal and off-limits for interference.* Controllers consume
those around them, assuming that others are as interested in working excessive
hours each week at the expense of families and children as they are. Their
formal rhetoric, as in the case of Perot, may stress family values, but rarely do
the organizations they run support those values. As early as possible, try to
establish some ground rules about work impinging on your personal time
and set limits beyond which you will not go. You may be willing to work late
some evenings, for example, but not on weekends. You may be willing to
travel half of the time, but not all of the time. Setting down these informal
parameters as soon as possible and resisting any change is crucial to keep a
controller from extending his tentacles beyond the normal workweek to
directing your private time as well.

Know the organizational rules and use them to your advantage. As skilled
generators and manipulators of rules, controllers have a begrudging respect
for others who exhibit the same flair. Know the organizational rules and
procedures for where you work. Get an organizational chart and employee
manual. Know the processes for sign-offs on projects and approval of
recruiting, purchasing, and contracting. Find loopholes whenever you can to
achieve your objectives.

*Do not challenge the controller directly, but do so through indirect slowdowns
and actions.* The thing that controllers like least is to lose control. A direct
challenge is a significant threat to a controller for it symbolizes and may be a
loss of control. If you do not plan to do what a controller who has direct
power over you wants you to do, a direct challenge is not well advised. Try
to circumvent the controller in some less direct way, using technicalities,
slowing down work on objectionable strategies, and engaging in passive rather
than overt resistance. Your long-term survival if you use these strategies
against a controller is not guaranteed, but if you use direct confrontation, it
most certainly is not.

*Talk with other employees to set up an informal organizational network within
the formal organization to share information and provide support.* Others may
have the same problems with the controller that you have. Informal networks
can provide information and support that you need to survive. Find out who
shares your views that sometimes the controller is misguided and out-of-
bounds. In this way, common strategies for minimizing the impact of

misguided controller directives without undermining reasonable and useful ones can be discussed. Controllers who eventually feel they have lost control because the organization is not responding as they wish it to will, like Perot did at GM, eventually go away.

NOTES

1. Gloria Borger and Jerry Buckley with David Gergen, Steven V. Roberts, Dorian Friedman, and Bureau Reports, "Perot Keeps on Going and Going . . . ," *U.S. News and World Reports* 114, no. 19 (May 17, 1993), pp. 37–47.

2. Todd Mason, *Perot: An Unauthorized Biography* (Homewood, IL: Dow Jones-Irwin, 1990), p. 3.

3. Joseph E. Persico, *Casey: From the OSS to the CIA* (New York: Viking, 1990), pp. 68, 231.

4. Bob Woodward, "Casey Found to have 'Misrepresented' Facts to Win Aid for Contras," *Washington Post*, November 19, 1987, p. A1.

5. John Barry, with Tony Clifton, Daniel Pedersen, Christopher Dickey, Ruth Marshall, Theodore Stranger, Fred Colman, Michael Meyer, John McCormick, Ginny Carroll, and Donna Foote, "Making of a Myth: The October Surprise," *Newsweek* (November 11, 1991), pp. 18–25.

6. "C.I.A.'s Casey Departs from Practice in Keeping Control of His Own Stocks," *New York Times*, November 23, 1981, p. A16.

7. Mason, p. 80.

8. Ibid., pp. 90–92.

9. Ibid., p. 83.

10. Doron P. Levin, *Irreconcilable Differences: Perot Versus General Motors* (Boston: Little, Brown, 1989), p. 250.

11. Levin, pp. 324–325.

IV

SNAPSHOTS OF
TOXIC LEADERS

The Enforcer

Thumbnail Sketch of the Enforcer (Consensus Leadership Style): Subservient and often second-in-command, enforcers are toxic leaders who need hierarchy, certainty, and money, and who echo the toxic leadership styles of those to whom they attach themselves and support. They seek consensus with the leaders to whom they report, often other toxic and transitional leaders, rather than with followers. Enforcers rarely achieve dominance in an organization but are instrumental to the success of others, especially street fighters, bullies, and absentee leaders.

HALLMARK CHARACTERISTICS OF THE ENFORCER

The enforcer is the Mafia hit man who carries out the orders of the godfather, even when they are unpleasant. The enforcer is also the solid administrator with a bureaucratic mentality that managed Hitler's Third Reich. Their consensus style, directed predominantly toward the leaders for whom they work, drives them to fulfill and even anticipate the desires of their bosses. In a more modern setting, Bob Haldeman and John Ehrlichman, whose actions in Watergate helped to bring down the Nixon presidency, were enforcers. So was Oliver North in the Reagan administration, whose subterfuge and secret negotiations of arms for hostages in the Iran-Contra affair blighted the Reagan presidency.

Usually enforcers are less colorful than those just mentioned, and even they became more colorful after their questionable activities and misdeeds became publicly known. Indeed, Oliver North used his notoriety in the Iran-Contra affair to become a spokesperson for the right wing of the Republican Party and to acquire funds to launch his 1994 campaign in Virginia for the U.S.

Senate. In his spellbinding testimony before Congress in which he explained under oath his role in the Iran-Contra affair, North appeared in uniform, although he seldom wore his uniform to work, shrouded in both the cloth and the rhetoric of patriotism—his justification for earlier defying the law and lying to both that body and the public.[1]

More typically, enforcers, despite wielding considerable power, are gray, bland, and almost invisible. They may shuffle back and forth from their offices to their cars before most employees have come to work in the morning and after most have left in the evening, their shoulders hunched, burdened by their jobs, carrying valises and briefcases stuffed with papers. Most of the enforcers surrounding Richard Nixon and associated with Watergate have largely disappeared from the national collective consciousness, including John Dean, Bob Haldeman, and John Ehrlichman.

Enforcers will deny that there is anything inherently evil about themselves. They do not need to kick sleeping dogs, beat their wives, or (unlike the bully) run around the organization threatening to fire employees. Enforcers often claim to be family oriented. Thus, the families of Watergate defendants Haldeman and Dean showed up daily, glued to their sides, at the Watergate hearings.[2] Maureen Dean, or "Mo," as she was called by John Dean and eventually the press and the nation, a stunningly attractive but seemingly unflappable blond, was particularly the subject of national attention. North also presented himself as a family man, stating that he always attended church with his family when in town. Acknowledging that he missed many family dinners while working at the National Security Council (NSC) and spent many weekends in the office, North nonetheless claims he was in bible study group with his family and took his son camping on the Appalachian Trail and canoeing on the Shenandoah and Potomac rivers.[3] Even Sammy "the Bull" Gravano, the enforcer for the "teflon mafia don," John Gotti, head of the Gambino family in New York, showed some family-oriented domestic skills. Sammy shopped and cooked for his fellow mobsters when awaiting the orders to proceed on a 1985 Christmastime hit on "Big" Paul Costellano, the "Boss of Bosses."[4]

Yet enforcers become evil on occasion and do evil things when they work for evil people. If busybodies are like megaphones, magnifying the rumors that they hear, then enforcers are like telephones, transmitting almost exactly what their superior desires. North reflected the Cold War "evil empire" attitude of the Reagan administration, willing and eager to combat communism in the Nicaraguan jungles of Central America against the wishes of Congress, and even though doing so required selling arms to Iran. North also carried out a secret propaganda operation in Nicaragua using congressionally prohibited federal funds, working through the State Department's Office of

Public Diplomacy for Latin America, and funneled weapons, supplies, money, and military intelligence to the contras.[5]

North's actions were compatible with Reagan's philosophy, and indeed, Reagan secretly approved the first shipment of one hundred U.S. TOW missiles to Iran, using Israel as an intermediary.[6] Independent counsel Lawrence Walsh, appointed to investigate the Iran-Contra affair, found it inconceivable that Reagan would have allowed the delivery of planeloads of arms to Iran without release of American hostages held in Iran, presumably the intent of the arms deal, without knowing that the ayatollah, Khomeni, had agreed to supply the contras.[7]

Similarly, the cover-up by enforcers around Richard Nixon reflected his feisty "fight like hell" to stay in office attitude. As the trouble surrounding Watergate mounted, so did Nixon's resolve to defeat it. The nation was shocked to discover that the eighteen-and-a-half-minute gap in the taped conversation between Nixon and Haldeman three days after the Watergate break-in was not the accident of an absent-minded secretary, but rather was the result of at least five and possibly as many as nine separate manual erasures.[8] Plainly, the president's attitude had been manifested in the cover-up undertaken by his enforcers.

In the Gambino family, so clearly did enforcers reflect the intent of the godfather (toxic leader) they served, that they did not always know whom they were going to "hit," "whack," or "rub out"—all euphemisms for killing—before they set out on the task. When Gotti laid out plans to his cabal to make a major hit, some enforcers—Sammy Gravano, Angelo Ruggiero, Frank DeCicco—knew the target because they were aware of the politics within the crime family. But others, namely Eddie Lino, "Fat" Sally Scala, Vinnie Artuso, Johnny Carneglia, Tony "Roach" Rampino, Joey Watts, and Iggy Alogna, could not guess until moments before the hit at what the "serious business" was and who was to be whacked. Gotti was that sure of the loyalty of his enforcers and their willingness to carry out his orders, even when it meant risking their lives.[9]

If enforcers work for trustworthy leaders, they are fairly accurate, detail-oriented paper pushers who strive for consensus with their bosses, and who are loyal to the organization and the system. But trustworthy leaders can do better than enforcers for their second-in-command and close advisors. Trustworthy leaders are not satisfied with just paper pushers and systems maintenance people. Trustworthy leaders are not afraid of challenge, innovation, new ideas, change, or Grade A people. In fact, trustworthy leaders are invigorated by and even demand these things. Thus, trustworthy leaders who inherit enforcers from predecessors often, and in as nondisruptive a fashion as possible, eventually ease them out.

Most enforcers work for and with other toxic leaders. Enforcers can work for any other type of toxic leader, but most likely work for street fighters, the type who most need gangs of loyal employees willing to act on their commands without questioning. Enforcers can also work for bullies, although no one likes working for bullies very much. The very vicious and volatile nature of bullies means they are capable of turning on anyone in an angry temper tantrum, even the most loyal and devoted enforcer. Nixon, at times, evidenced characteristics of a bully, and his enforcers assumed his paranoid attitudes and siege mentality, viewing the press, other politicians, and even the public at times as the enemy.

Plainly, John Gotti was an ill-tempered bully. In addition to the power-grabbing hit on Paul Costellano, he ordered many other hits. In one awkward moment for the Federal Bureau of Investigation (FBI) and an embarrassing moment for John Gotti, the FBI saved his life. The Newark FBI had placed a social club run by the rival Genovese family under surveillance. The family was angry at Gotti because of his hit on Castellano. The head of the Genovese family himself, Vincent "the Chin" Gigante, was also fearful Gotti was going to make a run on the New Jersey construction unions that the Genovese family controlled and ordered the hit on Gotti and his brother. Genovese enforcers, knowing that the men's room of their social club might be bugged, met in the ladies' room to plan the hit, but the Newark FBI had bugged it as well. Thus, the FBI was placed in the awkward position of preventing a murder and informing Gotti of the planned hit.[10]

Gotti's reaction was pure rage and meanness, and for once, his enforcers refused to carry out his order to "kill the fuck!" In bully-like fashion, Gotti was vengeful and ferocious, kicking over chairs, slamming his thick fists into walls, and ranting nonstop. Gigante, the Genovese family head, had surrounded himself with so many bodyguards that it would require a "battalion" to take him out, and even then, success was doubtful. Finally, Gotti regained composure and ordered the next most reprehensible act of revenge—a hit on Gigante's underboss, Jimmy Rotondo, who was shot dead in his car and left with a bag of rotting fish. Gotti further took out his rage on a retarded kid who spooked him in the neighborhood of his social club, the Bergin. The kid, William Ciccone, was fascinated with the club and would stand outside staring at it for hours. Shortly after the hit on Rotondo, Gotti's enforcers stormed out of the club and began beating Ciccone with baseball bats, cracking his bones until he crumbled. He was later discovered with a bullet in his head, the price for spooking Gotti after the aborted Gigante plan.[11]

In Sammy "the Bull," however, Gotti had an enforcer whose brutality practically equalled his own. Indeed, Gotti had known Gravano, "the Bull," only casually for ten years, but sought him out as an enforcer when he decided to make a hit on Castellano. Gravano had a reputation for two characteristics Gotti used—he was greedy and he liked to kill. A "stone-cold iceman," Gravano killed his brother-in-law. First, the brother-in-law, Nicky Scibetta, a childhood friend as well as a relative, had borrowed money from Gravano and then refused to repay it. To allow even a relative to get away with that was a bad precedent and bad business. Second, his wife's brother had begun wearing an earring and colored his hair, so that Sammy's friends were teasing him about "being in love" with Nicky. Sammy shot his friend twice in the back of the head at close range, chopped up the body, and buried the incriminating evidence around the neighborhood. The plan went slightly awry when one day the Scibetta family was watching television and their dog trotted in with Nicky's hand in its mouth. Unable to find the rest of the body, the family made a silk-lined coffin for the hand and buried it with sacred rites.[12] By the time the government brought Sammy's hoodlum career to a close, he had killed nineteen men.[13]

Absentee leaders also need enforcers, almost as much as bullies and street fighters. Since absentee leaders devote little attention to the job, enforcers must run the organization. In the absence of a second level of enforcers with at least some self-interest in the well-being of the absentee leader, and in the absence much of the time of the absentee leader himself, the organization would rapidly disintegrate into chaos and virulent conflict if someone were not taking care of organizational business. Without enforcers, no one would buffer the absentee leader from jockeying street fighters and bullies and other toxic leaders immediately below. The close proximity of the absentee leader to toxic leader attacks from below would result in so many wounds to the absentee leader that his tenure would be shortened. Thus, behind every absentee leader of long duration stands a loyal enforcer, buffering the absentee leader from attacks and minding the organizational store in a routine if unexciting manner.

Ronald Reagan manifested characteristics of an absentee leader. Supporting his presidency were many enforcers, including the troika of the first administration, consisting of James Baker, Michael Deaver, and Edwin Meese. But below the troika in the first administration, and even more powerful in the second administration when the troika had been replaced by chief-of-staff Donald Regan, stood a second tier of enforcers, including Oliver North. North's comparatively low rank in the marines plus his personality made him ideal for his White House job, since the constraints of being a career military officer prevented him from being a direct threat to the political enforcers and others who worked in the Reagan White House. During that period when North worked for the National Security Council in the Reagan administration, his enforcer role enabled him to become the most powerful lieutenant colonel in U.S. history.

For enforcers, street fighters and absentee leaders are the most attractive of bosses. Under successful street fighters, enforcers gain and share in the street fighter's power, a power they would not otherwise have. They gain the thrill of victory from being on a winning team (at least in the short run) and close to the seat of power. The enforcers surrounding Lyndon Johnson, a president who manifested street fighter tendencies at various points, shared in the thrill of passing his Great Society and civil rights programs.

Under absentee leaders, enforcers have the delegated power of the organizational chieftain, but are not fully responsible or accountable for it. Given the absentee leader's general lack of interest in daily operations, enforcers must divine how the absentee leader would have acted in the same circumstances. The enforcer may even consult the absentee leader, but get only vague or half-formulated directives. The enforcer may have to interpret these partially developed directives, much like an ancient disciple visiting an oracle must subsequently interpret even the slightest sign from the oracle for significant meaning about how to conduct earthly affairs. Needless to say, this mode of operation leaves the enforcer with a lot of discretion. North, as the nation subsequently learned via national television, made maximum use of the discretion Ronald Reagan's absentee leadership allowed him.

Under absentee leaders, unlike street fighters, enforcers have considerable leeway to make decisions as they like as long as those decisions do not contradict the broad philosophy of the absentee leader or make the absentee leader look bad. When the enforcer makes bad decisions, however, subordinates are unclear about exactly who gave the order. The lines of accountability become amazingly blurred. The Tower report on Iran-Contra showed North's world to be a shady international network of "ships, planes, intelligence agents, corporate shells, and Swiss bank accounts."[14]

Rarely, however, do enforcers make many independent decisions, particularly bold ones. While Sammy "the Bull," for example, was fully capable of brutal murder, his choice of targets, by and large, did not upset the existing dons, nor his own position within the family. It was up to Gotti to challenge the power structure and order the hit that would propel him and those around him to be the "Boss of Bosses," the very pinnacle of Mafia power. North's actions in Iran-Contra, for all their boldness and illegality, perpetuated existing administration policy that Congress had tried unsuccessfully to curtail.

The natural instinct of enforcers is to kick hard decisions downward to heads of subunits below them, or upward in some instances to the toxic leader. The one characteristic that most typifies their consensual mode of operation is "rubber stamp." Enforcers put their stamp of approval on decisions moving in both directions—both those moving downward, emanating from the absentee leader or other type of toxic leader at the top of the organization, and those moving upward, originating in lower ranks. Enforcers do not care much about substance, but they do care deeply about the process of organization and their own place within the hierarchy. Thus, enforcers are tabulae rasae upon which other toxic leaders and malcontents can write.

Having rubber stamped most decisions made elsewhere, the principles of enforcers have the consistency of their stamp—rubber. Enforcers will bend and flex their principles to accommodate others. Sometimes they are so accommodating that their principles have been bent so far out of shape as to be unrecognizable. At some point in their careers, usually when they have been discharged, dismissed, or brought up on charges for acts committed under some malicious toxic leader, enforcers sit down and shake their heads, wondering how they got to this point of decline and ruin.

The answer, of course, is slowly, incrementally, bit by bit, flexing a little more each day to accommodate the toxic leader above, or to relieve pressure from and retain dominance over the struggling toxic leaders and malcontents below. Since enforcers are not introspective and do not contemplate the big picture, they fail to notice these daily changes or to speculate about their implications for the long-run futures of both the organization and themselves.

The flexibility of enforcers, as well as their commitment to their place in the process over substance leads to one of the more treacherous aspects of enforcers: if pressed hard enough, they will rat on the toxic leader bosses they serve. Indeed, Sammy "the Bull" turned out to be the star witness at the government's trial of Gotti for five murders. It was Gotti's third trial, having escaped on technicalities and jury bribes on earlier efforts to convict him. When Gotti, Sammy, and Frankie Locascio were arrested, the government played a tape for Sammy that showed Gotti was angry at him for hoarding profits for his own company, and called Sammy stupid. The tape implied that Gotti might order a hit on his own enforcer. Sammy brooded for eight months in prison and decided that if he beat the government's rap, he would have to whack twelve people to feel safe. If he didn't beat the rap, he would be locked away forever. That's when he decided to cut a deal.

Sammy had personal experience with rats. Not long before his own arrest, Sammy went to Gotti to request permission to kill Eddie Garafolo, one of the guys on his crew, under the mere suspicion that Eddie was ratting to the government. Sammy's evidence was that Garafolo had gotten a light three-month sentence and had been given two furloughs while doing time. Gotti gave Sammy permission and Sammy shot Eddie in the eyeball and the mouth to show others what happened to rats. Little did he know at the time that when backed up against the wall, he would soon be standing in Eddie's shoes.[15]

Likely Sources of Sense of Inadequacy for the Enforcer

Enforcers operate at Maslow's level two, below the typical operational level of absentee leaders, busybodies, and controllers, for their primary concern is with and about security. Enforcers feel insecure. They want to feel secure. They need the organizational structure to provide them with the shelter they need for security and are fearful that they could not survive without it. Generally, they are right.

Mostly, enforcers are economically insecure and crave economic security, as much as power and prestige. Because of this, the loyalty of enforcers can be bought more readily than that of most other toxic leaders and of other employees in general. To gain money and security, which they could not acquire so readily in other positions, enforcers will put up with and go along with unfair and even degrading policies against which others will rebel.

Money is a primary incentive for enforcers. Nothing will substitute for it. Indeed, other pleasures, such as sexual conquests, drinking, and conspicuous consumption are but distractions from making advances within the organization that will bring more money. For enforcers, the point of money is not necessarily to spend it in conspicuous consumption, although they can be big spenders when they feel they must. Rather, the point of money is to have it. To have it is to be secure and sheltered. To not have it is to be insecure and unsheltered.

Money was the enticement for Gravano that Gotti used to get "the Bull" to join his ranks for the Costellano hit. While North stated that he only wished to serve his country, he successfully used his enforcer role to serve his own economic interests, raising hundreds of thousands of dollars through speaking, writing, and solicitation for funds from conservative sources, rising in a short time from a modest lieutenant colonel's salary to the income of a millionaire. Both John Dean, a Watergate enforcer, and his wife tried to cash in on their roles in the downfall of a president by writing books for money.

When enforcers do engage in conspicuous consumption, it is begrudgingly and usually with more taste than when other toxic leader types, including street fighters, do the same. For street fighters, the point of conspicuous consumption is to impress subordinates and their loyalty to the "winning gang," made more appealing by big money splash and flash. For enforcers, the reason to spend money is not to impress lowly underlings, but rather, to engage in more tasteful displays that impress higher level superiors in order to secure advancements and make more money.

Gravano, for example, made calculated decisions about how to maximize his money. At the time of his arrest with Gotti, Gravano had about a million and a half out "on the street." He sent out the order that everyone must keep paying on their accounts, backed up by a few underlings threatening key customers with death. If he were convicted, however, Gravano knew the incentive for customers to pay would be lessened or removed. After eight months in the Metropolitan Corrections Center when things looked bleak, Gravano made a calculated decision to discount the account balances in order to collect something on what was due. Something was better than nothing.

Nothing is more serious to the enforcer than money. Enforcers, more than any other toxic leader type, are salary slaves. When confronted with the prospect or reality of monetary adversity and financial ruin, street fighters will assume that what was once seized in gang battles can be seized again. Bullies will become bitter and live for wreaking revenge and havoc on the people they think brought them financial ruin. Enforcers, their sense of well being shattered to the very core, will weigh all the angles and then do whatever is necessary and within their power to prevent the ruin, including turning on those they once loyally served.

For some enforcers, particularly those highly placed in politics and the public sector where salaries are capped and relatively low compared to their counterparts in the private sector, the promise of money for loyal service is not immediate, but rather is realized when enforcers "cash in" on their positions and contacts in the organization after leaving. People who have worked in the highest levels of government can often parlay their proximity to power into lucrative lobbying, consulting, and power broker roles after leaving, reaping financial gains far beyond what they might have achieved without first serving in their enforcer roles. Even those accused and/or convicted of wrongdoing hold the prospect of writing memoirs and "kiss and tell" books, earning royalties and speaking fees. North, in particular, ended up being rich because of his zealotry and excesses in his enforcer role, without which he might still be an officer of modest income in the U.S. Marine Corps.

Enforcers differ greatly in how much money it takes for them to begin to feel secure, or more accurately, to abate gnawing insecurity somewhat. In part, how much money it takes depends on the social class in which the enforcer was raised. But the social class of the family in which toxic leaders were raised is not a predictor of whether or not the toxic leader will become an enforcer in later life. Rather, a better predictor is the emphasis the family and immediate peer group, regardless of social class, placed on money.

Most enforcers were raised in a family where money was a defining measure of self-worth. Key figures, usually parents, in enforcer families from working class and lower origins saw money as a means for escape from their drudgery and insecurity. Middle-class parental figures may have felt they were only one or two paychecks away from an unhappy descent into lower social classes.

Upper-middle-class parents may have felt that money was the thing that made them more refined and better than the hoi polloi.

Another predictor of being an enforcer is the fact that the prospective toxic leader lacks or feels he lacks any other notable assets that would provide uniqueness and distinction. Thus, the enforcer sees adherence to and fitting into the organizational system as the major means of obtaining money and personal success, and sets out to fit into and manage the system better than all others. We see, then North unsuccessfully seeking to join the U.S. Senate in 1994 to belong to the organizational system he once decried as being too blind to see the country's best interest and too cowardly to act upon what they did see.

ENFORCERS AND THE ORGANIZATION

Operational Style and Tactics of the Enforcer

Enforcers are able to work with other, more flamboyant and egotistical toxic leaders because their primary motivation is money and security, not being the top leader in the organization. They are content with being number two. They notice how the top leader often gains unfavorable public attention, and receives criticism and attacks from those both outside and inside the organization. Being behind and below the top toxic leader reduces the number of these direct attacks.

The major threat of a disloyal enforcer to a top toxic leader is not that the enforcer will try to seize the top job. Rather, it is that the enforcer will be bought by some other more flamboyant toxic leader who does want the top job, and will help the competition overthrow the enforcer's boss. Because enforcers have little substantive interest beyond making the system work as well as possible and rising as high as possible within it, who is in the number one position is largely irrelevant to them, as long as their own position is secure. Thus, enforcers are often key actors in such overthrows of top toxic leaders as military coups, corporate board dismissals of chief executive officers, and hostile takeovers.

Like controllers, enforcers know the organizational rules and regulations well and use them to advantage. But enforcers have less personal investment in any particular policy and are more dispassionate about their actions. Enforcers are able to analyze the emotions and incentives of others through a largely disinterested view, as long as their own position and salaries are not involved. Enforcers provide a particularly valuable prism to more volatile, egotistical, and emotional top toxic leaders.

Enforcers are able executors of orders and message carriers. While enforcers would rather carry good messages than bad messages, they are mostly indifferent. They recognize that the organizational machinery crushes some people some of the time. While this is a regrettable fact of organizational life, to enforcers, it is a fact not easily changed or not changeable at all. As long as they are sufficiently confident in their own skills and abilities to avoid being crushed themselves, that others are is just part of the job. Enforcers can be delegated as "hit men" like Gravano to distribute punishments as well as "bag men" like North to distribute rewards and payoffs by toxic leaders higher up.

Impact of the Enforcer on the Organization

Enforcers represent the status quo in terms of their impact on the organization. Whatever the status quo is, enforcers support it. If the status quo is uplifting and progressive, the enforcers implement uplifting and progressive policies. But, if the status quo is organizational drift or decline, the enforcers implement drift- and decline-inducing policies.

The presence of relatively efficient enforcers may prop up an agency or corporation descending into organizational drift, by assuring that at least routine issues will be handled and routine decisions will be made. Of course, the outcome will be routine as well, doing little or nothing to correct for organizational drift. In organizations that have gone past drift and descended into decline, enforcers appear helpless to reverse the decline.

Enforcers are largely impartial to organizational decline as long as their own positions are secure. The infighting and battles between factions become spectator sports to many within the organization, including unaffected enforcers. When the infighting begins to threaten the well-being of enforcers themselves, however, they prove capable of swift and deadly action. The hit-man capacity they use on occasion to the benefit of their toxic leader can also be used to defend their own positions, in one of the few instances when enforcers make independent decisions.

Unlike other toxic leaders who generate organizational decline by their own actions, enforcers do not usually personally initiate behaviors that create factions and inter- and intrasubunit wars. Rather, enforcers merely preside over decline when it occurs, unwilling or unable to reverse it. Enforcers reflect and perpetuate whatever exists. When evil exists, enforcers reflect and perpetuate that as indifferently as good, and in their ambivalence and indifference to evil, become evil themselves.

Protecting Yourself Against an Enforcer

To a certain extent, all leaders must depend on loyal subordinates to achieve their goals for the organization. But enforcers go several steps beyond loyal subordinates to incorporate several of the "mals" that toxic leaders manifest, because they operate primarily at Maslow's level two. Several guidelines may help you protect yourself from the worst aspects of enforcers you may encounter in your organizational life.

Do not expect enforcers to challenge their toxic leader bosses unless offered a better deal. Since enforcers are motivated by security and money, often seeing the two synonymously, they will not readily challenge their current boss, even if you urge them to participate in an organizational coup against the top toxic leader. The major exception is when enforcers are offered a better deal. Unless you are capable of doing that and prepared to do so, do not expect enforcers to join you in some plot to overthrow a toxic leader at the top.

Do not come between enforcers and their money. Enforcers are serious about money for the security it provides. Note that one of the offenses on which North was convicted dealt not with his role in illegally selling arms under the table to an enemy holding U.S. hostages without release of the hostages, but rather, was accepting illegal gratuities—an electronic security and surveillance system for his house, so convinced was he that he had become the target of international terrorists. Enforcers who feel their security is threatened are capable of desperate deeds, so do not come between enforcers and their money if you can help it.

Use loyal enforcers to deliver messages to their bosses. Since enforcers are like telephone lines to the toxic leaders they serve, use them as such selectively. Know that telling an enforcer something is equivalent to telling the same thing to his boss.

Know that ultimately, enforcers can be bought. Enforcers, even the seemingly most loyal ones, can be bought. If you must do business with an enforcer, go with bounty in hand if you expect cooperation that transcends his boss's interest. Ultimately, enforcers, such as Sammy "the Bull," who rat on their bosses are also being "bought"—for a better deal, picking the best choice out of a series of bad options.

If you have an enforcer working for you, realize that your interests and the enforcer's interests are not identical, no matter how loyal the enforcer may seem. Should you at some future point find an enforcer under your supervision, the enforcer's interests will never be exactly identical to your own. It is easy, given the unquestioning loyalty enforcers seem to offer, to forget this. But enforcers are quiet when they are angry at the boss on whom their well-being depends, and bide their time until they can express it without self-harm. In the long-run, trustworthy leaders are better served by subordinates who question and criticize as well as support and praise. Those who think independently and are willing to offer a different perspective are the best subordinates to have.

NOTES

1. Philip Weiss, "Oliver North's Next War," *New York Times Magazine* (July 4, 1993), pp. 12–15, 33–37.

2. John W. Dean, III, *Blind Ambition: The White House Years* (New York: Simon and Schuster, 1976), pp. 377–378.

3. Oliver North with William Novak, *Under Fire: An American Story* (New York: Harper Collins, 1991), pp. 168–170.

4. Howard Blum, *Gangland: How the FBI Broke the Mob* (New York: Simon and Schuster, 1993), pp. 102–103.

5. Haynes Johnson, *Sleepwalking Through History: America in the Reagan Years* (New York: W. W. Norton, 1991), pp. 286–289.

6. Johnson, p. 290.

7. Scott Spencer, "Lawrence Walsh's Last Battle," *New York Times Magazine* (July 4, 1993), pp. 11, 28–33.

8. Elizabeth Drew, *Washington Journal: The Events of 1973–1974* (New York: Random House, 1975), pp. 166–167.

9. Blum, pp. 114–116.

10. Ibid., pp. 181–182.

11. Ibid., pp. 183–184.

12. Ibid., pp. 107–108.

13. Ibid., p. 339.

14. Ben Bradlee, Jr., *Guts and Glory: The Rise and Fall of Oliver North* (New York: Donald I. Fine, 1988), p. 483.

15. Blum, p. 306.

10

The Street Fighter

Thumbnail Sketch of the Street Fighter (Coordinating Leadership Style):
Egotistical and often charismatic, street fighters are toxic leaders with a
"king of the mountain" syndrome who are driven to dominate through
gang politics. Street fighters operate on gut level survival instincts, and
the principle of rewards and punishments for loyalty to their "gang,"
rather than to the organization as a whole. They coordinate through
rewards and punishments and their competitive vision of winning at
any cost. They solicit input from followers who can help with victory,
but readily smash any who challenge them or dissent. Street fighters can
be generous to those who show loyalty but vicious, exacting swift
retribution, to those who do not.

HALLMARK CHARACTERISTICS OF THE STREET FIGHTER

Street fighters are the most glamorous and exciting of all toxic leaders. They
exude a limited amount of personal charisma. They are the most like the
"gamesman" that has come to dominate modern corporations and the team
leaders who are trustworthy leaders with a coordinating style. Street fighters
at their best are like quarterbacks—building, cajoling, managing, and exhort-
ing others to contribute to the team.

Consider George Wallace, a street fighter who loomed large on the
American scene in the 1960s and 1970s. Wallace, the segregationist governor
of Alabama during the 1960s, generated almost a palpable excitement among
his constituents, helping them to "rediscover America" by standing up for
their right to be left in peace, now broken by federal intervention on civil

rights after almost one hundred years. Wallace launched his third party bid for the U.S. presidency in 1968 because, as he told his followers, "he had to win something." To his often downtrodden constituents watching him on television from their small town and rural residences, Wallace stood up to the "big-city slick-hair boys" for the "little people."[1]

Jesse Jackson, a disciple of the visionary civil rights leader, Martin Luther King, at times exhibited street fighter characteristics. Jackson joined the civil rights movement late and demanded that the movement people find a role for him. After King's assassination, Jackson founded PUSH-Excel, a program for motivating minority youth and discouraging drug use to propel himself to the national stage. His capacity to excite and energize crowds is legendary, urging them to chant "I am SOMEBODY," "A pearl, who could learn anything—in the WORLD."[2] Jackson's drive for legitimacy left him as hungry for the crowds as they were for him, a hunger that he expressed through superhuman drive and charisma, spellbinding oration and speech-making, and heart-rending fund raising.

Sometimes the charisma of the street fighter does not come across in large groups, but rather is evident in small groups and one-on-one interactions. Former president Lyndon Johnson also evidenced street fighter characteristics on occasion, but lacked the capacity to captivate a crowd in the same manner that Wallace and Jackson could. Rather, Johnson excelled at cornering friends and foes alike and giving them the famous "Johnson treatment," arguments so persuasive and a physical presence so compelling that those being subjected to this treatment simply could not say no. Johnson has been acclaimed as one of the most effective Senate majority leaders ever. Clark Clifford later said of Johnson that he knew his colleagues so well "he played the Democrats in the Senate the way a skilled harpist would play a harp. He knew which string to pull at a particular time and how far he could bring a fellow along."[3]

Like most street fighters, Johnson valued toughness. On the last night of Johnson's first Senate campaign, Lady Bird, his wife, was in an automobile accident that left her rattled and severely bruised. Yet she ignored her pain and attended the closing reception, borrowing clothes to wear to replace her torn dress and stockings. She did not mention her accident to Lyndon during the reception, and later when he discovered the injuries, he thought her performance was wonderful, exciting, and courageous.[4] Similarly, when Johnson was president, he was proud of his survival of a painful operation, lifting his shirt to show the nation his scars. Johnson thought he was demonstrating how tough he had been under the surgeon's knife, but the press blanched and saw it as a sign of being uncouth.

Another street fighter was Donald T. Regan, former head of the giant financial investment company Merrill Lynch, secretary of the Treasury during Ronald Reagan's first term, and White House chief of staff during the first part of Reagan's second term. Although from the Northeast and not California, Regan resembled the rough hewn self-made entrepreneurs of Reagan's kitchen cabinet who bankrolled his early political career more than his immediate predecessor as White House chief of staff, the more genteel James Baker. With roots in Irish Catholic Boston, Regan's father had been a Boston policeman. When Regan's brilliant brother died of peritonitis, the hopes and expectations of his parents fell upon him. Regan as a youth had been unruly but applied himself, earned a scholarship to Harvard, and went to work on Wall Street. Feisty and driven, Regan often beat his competition to the punch with innovations in the financial industry, becoming a multi-millionaire and head of Merrill Lynch.[5]

Despite their charisma in some settings and sometimes popular appeal, street fighters have an achilles heel that differentiates them irrevocably from trustworthy leaders who are also charismatic and team builders—they are afflicted with a fatal "king of the mountain" syndrome. They must be the leader, the top dog, the leader of the pack. Their unwavering need to be dominant produces power struggles when challenged and a pack mentality. This unwavering need to dominate, more than anything else, defines the street fighter.

Engaging in both hard-fought gubernatorial campaigns in his native state of Alabama and in bitter battles with the federal courts, George Wallace embraced what he, himself, termed, "fierce contact with life."[6] When Wallace first ran for governor in 1958 against John Patterson, he described himself as feeling "like a boxer dancing around the ring with no opponent," when Patterson's campaign strategists shielded him from the press.[7] Indeed, Wallace, despite being small in stature in his youth had been an avid boxer. He developed a reputation as such in his home county of Barbour, and at age fifteen, was known as "the Barbour Bantam." Wallace carried his love of fighting over to his political life. Running political races and fighting campaigns was the part of politics that he loved the most.

Wallace even reveled in clashing with hecklers, and describes how he handled his first hecklers, a group of school children in Columbiana, the home of one of his opponents. The children started to razz Wallace and to scream for Harrison, his opponent. Wallace responded that he knew that they had a fine candidate but if they would let him finish his speech, he would get out of town. Most of the children cheered and quieted down. A few boys remained rowdy, so Wallace promised to promote them to the second grade in exchange for their silence. This did not suffice, so Wallace upped the ante to closing down the school and achieved the desired effect.[8]

Wallace enjoyed putting on a show of power, attracting people who felt powerless and who had a very limited understanding of power.[9] Wallace enjoyed the image of defiance, even when there was no fight. During his 1958 gubernatorial campaign, Wallace, then a circuit court judge, had refused to turn over Barbour County voting records to the Civil Rights Commission, even when subpoened. He said he would instead turn them over to a grand jury, and that his actions were legal. Further, Wallace threatened to jail any agent who came to get the records. In a series of cat-and-mouse moves between Wallace and the federal courts, a contempt trial occurred. Surprisingly, Wallace was found not guilty, since Wallace had submitted the records to the grand jury, and was found to have assisted, through devious means, the Civil Rights Commission in getting the records. Rather than pleasure at the outcome of the contempt trial, Wallace was furious, for his image of deviance had been punctured.[10]

Wallace continued to project street fighter defiance and a determination to be top dog even when he was the underdog in his most famous move, his stand in the schoolhouse door at the University of Alabama in June 1963. Wallace met with President Kennedy at the thirtieth anniversary of the Tennessee Valley Authority and Kennedy tried to dissuade the scrappy governor from persisting in his resistance to a federal order to desegregate the university. Wallace responded that he would personally bar any attempt to enroll blacks. Wallace then appeared on the national television show *Meet the Press*, heightening expectations and visibility. When two black students, accompanied by Nicholas J. Katzenbach, the U.S. assistant attorney general who arrived to enroll the students, Wallace was waiting with a microphone and public address system in the doorway through which the students must pass.

In high drama broadcast to the nation, Katzenbach served Wallace with a cease and desist order from President Kennedy to stop interfering with enrollment. Wallace read a prepared statement that claimed the people of Alabama had the right to operate its public schools as they saw fit, and that he, Wallace, would not step aside. Katzenbach left to have lunch with the students, and President Kennedy immediately federalized the Alabama National Guard. Four hours later, the General of the Alabama Guard returned to inform Wallace that he must step aside. Wallace did, but not before he read another statement pledging to continue the fight against federal interference.[11] The students enrolled without further incident. Wallace's street fighter image was now indelibly stamped on the nation's consciousness.

Jackson also had a strong drive to be "king of the mountain," striving to replace King as leader of the civil rights movement when the creator of the "I have a dream" speech was shot in Memphis. Even before his death, however, King began to complain to Reverend James Bevel, the minister who recommended Jackson to him, that Jackson "had the ability to prostitute a race for one's own self-aggrandizement," and "to build an empire at the expense of our people."[12]

Others complained that Jackson was hardworking and smart, but also manipulative. His tendency to grab the limelight was revealed in the "bloody shirt" incident. Jackson, according to eye witnesses, was present in the Memphis courtyard when King was shot, but was not near to him. Yet later, when others were making funeral arrangements for King, Jackson disappeared and reappeared before television cameras in Chicago, wearing a shirt he claimed was bloodied when he cradled the dying leader in his lap.

Eye witnesses say that Ralph Abernathy actually held the dying King and that Jackson was not close. Jackson lambasted the Chicago City Council that those who would not have welcomed King would have the blood on his shirt on their heads. Fellow civil rights workers saw Jackson's actions as an image-making grab for power and the limelight in his attempt to self-anoint himself successor to King, shoving aside Andrew Young, who was being groomed by King for the role.[13]

Those who knew Jackson well knew that he was always eager to be noticed and in charge. Born to an unmarried sixteen-year-old mother, his blood father, Noah Robinson, Sr., lived next door for a while, and eventually had a much more affluent lifestyle. Even the marriage of his mother to his stepfather, Charles Henry Jackson, did not mute Jackson's drive to achieve legitimacy through achievement. At five years old, even before he knew his ABCs, he announced to his blood father that he would be a preacher, and by the time he was a teenager, proclaimed to Noah, Sr. that he was a born leader.[14]

Those close to Jackson claim that he only shared power once in his life—with his half-brother, Noah, Jr., in Chicago, when both men were still in their late twenties. Noah, Jr., a graduate of Wharton and a financial whiz, was enticed to Chicago to help Jesse run Operation Breadbasket. But after a year, a bitter split occurred and the two did not speak to each other for five years. During that time, revenge was the driving force behind Noah. Jackson eventually initiated a reconciliation, but never again shared power within any organization to the same extent. His organization, PUSH, was criticized for mostly pushing Jesse, often opening a chapter in a new town with considerable fanfare and little follow-through.

When Jackson ran for president in 1984, only three major black elected officials left Mondale to back his campaign—Mayor Richard Hatcher of Gary, Indiana; Mayor Marion Barry of Washington, D.C.; and Mayor Kenneth Gibson of Newark, New Jersey. When he ran again in 1988, Willie Brown, speaker of the California Assembly, pledged support on the condition that Jackson share at least some power by hiring a campaign manager.[15] When accused of having no one around capable of telling him when the emperor had no clothes, Jackson responded that "big egos are not a problem if it correlates with their intelligence. The only problem is if they have a Cadillac ego and a bicycle brain."[16]

Johnson plainly exhibited a "king of the mountain" syndrome in his political campaigns. Running for the House of Representatives in 1937 from the tenth district in Texas, Johnson became the youngest member of the Texas delegation, with only two other members of the 435-seat House as young as he.[17] In his 1948 U.S. Senate race against Coke Stevens, Johnson was widely accused of having "stolen" the race by fraud at the ballot box. Before the race, Johnson minimized his previous support of the New Deal, running against communists and labor unions, and picking a public fight with President Harry Truman early in the race to erase his image as an FDR "yes" man. Even so, he won that pivotal race in his career by less than one-tenth of one percent of the votes, 494,191 to 494,104.[18] During his years in Congress, once his seat was secured, Johnson concentrated on accumulating a king-size fortune through a communications and financial empire. Born the son of an impoverished father, one biographer estimates Johnson's family assets, when he entered the White House, to be approximately $20 million, making him possibly the richest man to become president, up to that time.[19]

It was Johnson's Vietnam policy, however, where his need for dominance and unwillingness to relinquish power and acknowledge a mistake or defeat had its greatest impact. Johnson impressed both journalists and advisors with his deeply felt resolve not to lose in Vietnam.[20] Biographer Doris Kearns contends that the decision to escalate U.S. involvement in 1965 was likely inevitable, given Johnson's nature and convictions. Johnson believed that a communist victory in that distant country where, previously, years of unsuccessful war had almost sundered the French republic, would be a great defeat for the United States.[21]

When in doubt about what to do, Johnson's tendency was to fight, saying later in justification of his decision to escalate bombing that he felt "doing nothing was more dangerous than doing something."[22] Once mired in war, Johnson resisted withdrawal in the absence of victory, saying he did not want to be the first U.S. president to lose a war.

Donald Regan also exhibited a need to dominate in his considerable ego, disdain for politicians, lack of understanding of the political role that Nancy Reagan played in her husband's career and administration, and importation of a group of "yes" aides known as "the mice" from the Treasury Department to the White House—all fatal to his effectiveness as White House chief of staff.[23] Having little respect for the power that women can wield, Regan got into struggles with two powerful women in Republican circles. In addition to his increasingly cold and eventually hostile interactions with Nancy Reagan, Regan began a battle to oust Margaret M. Heckler, a former congresswoman from Massachusetts, out of her cabinet position as secretary of health and human services. Regan lost the street fight of his career when Nancy galvanized the president to replace Regan. Ronald Reagan said that Nancy and others reported that because of Regan's outsized ego, handling people summarily, and forcing everyone who wanted to see the president to go through him first, White House morale was bad.[24] Regan felt he became the scapegoat for the Iran-Contra affair.[25]

Many street fighters are more successful than popular. Street fighters will self-destruct rather than gracefully relinquish the reigns of power, even when their demise is inevitable. Many street fighters are removed from power abruptly. Wallace was shot in Laurel, Maryland during the 1972 presidential race. Jackson was removed by the Southern Christian Leadership Council from Operation Breadbasket in the early 1970s, prompting him to start his own organization, PUSH. Johnson announced in March of 1968 that he would not stand for a second term of the presidency in the wake of national turmoil and protest over his Vietnam policy. Regan was abruptly dismissed from his position as chief of staff under Reagan.

Because they refuse to relinquish power, street fighters make elaborate arrangements to continue their rule in fact if not in law when they are temporarily removed from office. The gangster who continues to run his illegal operations from prison may be such a street fighter. So is the CEO who cannot tolerate the idea of no longer being in power and arranges to have a weak stoolie appointed president, even as he himself is being pushed up to be chairman of the board. Politicians such as George Wallace, who run their wives in their stead when they are legally prohibited from retaining office, are also street fighters. Smart underlings know enough to realize that they should not challenge these arrangements, even when across time the arrangements become less and less tenable, until the reality of long distance street fighter rule fades well into fiction.

Street fighters can be magnanimous when on top and things are going well, and as vicious as they are magnanimous when their top positions are threatened and things are going badly. Nothing will rile the street fighter more than a serious challenge to his authority, but by virtue of their personalities, street fighters generate challenges. The personality of street fighters is to organize gangs for competition and combat. Wallace controlled his campaign organizations. Jackson organized his often unruly followers. Johnson combatted communists and organized legislative coalitions. Regan controlled his "mice." To facilitate gang and coalition building, the street fighter needs enemies to attack, in a slightly more expanded version of scapegoating. Eventually, after seeing enemies even where none exist, the street fighter's behavior generates the very enemies he needs.

Street fighters adopt a simple, self-centered view of the world, placing everyone into one of two categories. The first category consists of good people worthy of rewards with obviously good judgment and the well-being of the organization at heart who support the street fighter. The second category consists of bad people deserving of punishment with terrible judgment out to undermine the organization who do not support the street fighter. The street fighter's view of organizational politics, and indeed, of life in general, never gets more complicated than this. The entire world is either for him or against him, and as long as the street fighter has power (forever, if the street fighter had his way), fates will be determined accordingly.

Street fighters may, for a period, generate new ideas, programs, and products. As long as they are king of their current organizational mountain, they do not care if others put forth new ideas, develop new products, or implement change. Indeed, street fighters are the most change oriented of all the toxic leaders. Thus, Wallace, the segregationist, eventually appointed blacks to government positions and distributed state spending and benefits in a manner to win black votes when doing so was politically expedient. Jackson created new organizations and new strategies for advancing the economic interests of blacks. With his Great Society and War on Poverty programs, Johnson generated the greatest social policy innovations since the New Deal. Regan pioneered many financial innovations, including the elimination of fixed commissions for brokers and inventing cash management accounts, a revolutionary practice that bashed traditional barriers between banking and investment services by allowing investment customers to write checks against their brokerage accounts.

While controllers are also at times not fearful of change, their overwhelming need to control all aspects of daily operations, to rarely delegate, and to claim all new ideas as their own eventually stifles innovation. Street fighters do not have any of these flaws. They do not need to control all aspects of daily operation, will willingly delegate, and give credit to others who generate new ideas, as long as their own dominant positions are not threatened. Street fighters like to see those below them producing, so they can claim credit not for any specific act, but for inspiring productive people. But ultimately, street fighters, because they think winning is all that matters and technical skills and specific knowledge bases are below them, run squarely into the Peter Principle—rising to a level where they are incompetent. Indeed, Johnson's lack of attention to regular intelligence and foreign policy reports and failure to develop an advisory network that assured he would be aware of such details contributed to his downfall.

Even if street fighters were performing competently initially, they invariably push their organization in new directions and ventures that assure the street fighter will run up against major personal limitations. They push the organization when they have competed victoriously with all the major factions or gangs in their current setting and need new gangs to fight.

Street fighters are driven to make organizational turf conquests. More than any other toxic leader, street fighters define their success and personal performance in terms of the magnitude of organizational turf they control. They are empire builders, and they must be building an empire or defending their empire from attack, or they will die. Maintaining an empire bores them: Johnson was much better building a legislative empire by passing new programs than he was at overseeing their administration; Wallace preferred the thrill of campaigning to the boredom of government; and Jackson practiced free-form politics, eschewing the mundaneness of holding office. Maintaining an empire provides no battle, no challenge, no fun.

When limitations are broached, and as perceptions that the street fighter is incompetent and no longer performing adequately grow and spread, the street fighter becomes more and more defensive. His former magnanimousness rapidly shifts into meanness. The attacks the street fighter formerly reserved for members of competing factions will be turned on members of his own. Where rewards were once passed out freely, punishments are now inflicted just as freely. That neither rewards nor punishments are strongly tied to more objective criteria of organizational performance does not bother or even occur to the street fighter. In the mind of the street fighter, loyalty based rewards and punishments *are* tied to employee contributions to the organization, for the street fighter eventually totally personalizes his leadership role and function, equating his own welfare and continuation to the welfare and continuation of the whole organization.

The street fighter is emotionally outraged when others challenge this philosophy and his decisions based upon it, for he perceives himself to be a good and just leader who sacrifices for the organization. Thus, the street fighter, more than any other toxic leader, engages in self-deception as much or more than he deceives others. It is the street fighter's unwavering belief that he is right, and that support for him is right for the organization, that allows this toxic leader to attract and manipulate organizational gang members.

Likely Sources of Sense of Inadequacy for the Street Fighter

The street fighter is affected by "small man sickness." This sickness comes in two varieties—physical and emotional. The physical variety is literally trying to overcome being physically small in a world that values bigness. Sometimes called the Napoleonic complex, those afflicted are aggressive and competitive to show that they are just as good as those who are bigger—indeed, that they are better.

The physical variety is aware that tall men start out at significantly higher salaries and have enhanced chances of promotions. The physical variety knows from long childhood and adolescent experience, where they were treated differently and unfavorably by sole virtue of being smaller, that it is an unfair world. Furthermore, the normal avenues that might otherwise be available to accommodate their street fighting instincts are often precluded. Unless they are minority and born in a ghetto, which most middle-class leaders are not, they cannot join actual street gangs. Their physical size precludes them from becoming a quarterback, nor does size allow them to play basketball, the other sport where teams are close knit and leadership plays a major role.

But rather than accept this, the street fighter develops an "I'll show them!" attitude and then launches a lifelong battle to do so. The street fighter hates being treated insignificantly or unimportantly, and pursues the reverse relentlessly—being top dog, mountain king. If the street fighter cannot look down on others physically, then he will do so organizationally. The street fighter figuratively stands on the backs of others to achieve the heights he could not do so literally.

George Wallace was a politician who personified the small man as street fighter. In his public life, he excelled at attacking others, making electrifying speeches and rallying whole crowds who identified with the need to tackle "the big boys" of American life—the corporate magnates, the newspaper and television barons, the power structure in Washington, D.C., and for that matter, just about anybody.

From the other end of the social spectrum, Robert Kennedy, also relatively small, shared many of the same street fighter tendencies. His brother and president, Jack Kennedy, was relatively tall and exhibited strong hedonist tendencies, at times potentially jeopardizing national security by sharing a girlfriend, Judith Exner, with a Mafia don. But Jack recognized the street fighter instincts in his physically smaller and younger brother, and made Bobby a trusted lieutenant as Attorney General. Bobby filled the role admirably by taking on the Mafia, a major crime organization previously ignored for the most part by J. Edgar Hoover's FBI.

The lifelong battle of street fighters to combat a sense of smallness by ascending organizations drives them to do whatever is necessary to achieve success. Unlike bullies, who have a deep-seated need to hurt others, street fighters have no such need. But street fighters will do whatever it takes to ascend to the organizational pinnacle. If ascent can be achieved by playing within bounds and rewarding others, then okay. But if ascent can only be achieved by playing out of bounds and punishing others, then so be it. Winning is, after all, the American creed, and the point. Losers are nothing. Winners are everything. Plainly, to the street fighter, the point is to win.

The second variety of street fighter is not necessarily physically small as an adult, but still thinks of himself as once small in some psychological sense, and has developed the same "I'll show them by being king of the mountain" drive. Indeed, Lyndon Johnson was quite tall, but remembered his whole life the smallness he felt as a poor child and youth in Texas with a relatively ne'er-do-well father. Growing up to be a physically tall adult was not enough to compensate for this childhood sense of inferiority and social smallness, nor to curb the tremendous street fighter drive to overcome it that emerged. This drive propelled Johnson's decisions about Vietnam, including his willingness to order secret missions into neutral countries and inflated body counts. As tacit and begrudging acknowledgement of one street fighter to another, Johnson could not stand Bobby Kennedy. Little wonder because the two were too much alike.

Growing up, Regan was smaller and more unruly than his older, scholastically gifted brother. Only when his brother died was he called on to fill his brother's shoes—big shoes that likely made him feel small at the time and later relative to the task at hand. Similarly, Jackson developed a lifelong rivalry with his more fair-skinned and intellectually bright half-brother, Noah Robinson, Jr. Jackson used to peer through the fence from his modest home to the bigger home where his half-brother led a more privileged life.

Street fighters operate primarily at Maslow's level two. They are concerned about safety—and for good reason, since the battles in which street fighters engage are high visibility, risky events. George Wallace and Robert Kennedy were shot. Johnson eventually barricaded himself in the White House and visited mostly military bases to protect himself from attacks by war protesters and the press. Street fighters do not lack for enemies who wait for them to weaken and fall.

STREET FIGHTERS AND THE ORGANIZATION

Operational Style and Tactics of the Street Fighter

Street fighters use "buddy" politics in their organizations to build friendship networks. The networks, in turn, become the basis for building support groups for the street fighter. High-level street fighters often have enforcers that manage the more mundane details and handle unpleasant tasks. But it is the charisma and appeal of the street fighter, along with his wiliness and determination to win that brings supporters to his faction.

Having experienced the insensitivities of others as a youth, the street fighter is nonetheless sensitive enough to figure out the main drives and concerns of most of his immediate supporters. The street fighter feeds those drives and addresses the concerns, as long as doing so does not threaten his own leadership position. The street fighter is not miserly, and will freely disperse monies to placate and motivate supporters. Conversely, the street fighter will deny money to opponents, but not out of miserliness. Rather this denial is punishment for not supporting the street fighter, or worse, for challenging his control. No punishment is too petty for the street fighter, including denial of parking privileges.

Street fighters tend to have a coffee klatch, a lunch bunch, or a drinking crowd, even among supporters. These are particularly loyal and devoted followers who have benefitted from the street fighter's tenure in top leadership. Some would not be as highly placed on merit alone and owe their jobs to the street fighter. Regan's "mice" are examples of subordinates who owed their jobs to their loyalty to their street fighter boss as much as to other factors and talents. Some subordinates have been allowed to earn money on the side or to get special deals at work not given to other employees that have been financially lucrative. Some have been advanced, skirting organizational rules or ignoring them totally. These beneficiaries are the supporters who socialize and "pal around" with the street fighter on a regular basis. But since their loyalty is based as much on special benefits as on the personal appeal of the street fighter, when the street fighter inevitably takes on one too many battles and is removed or eased out of power, the loyalty of these supporters fades as fast as do the special benefits.

Impact of the Street Fighter on the Organization

Street fighters are not particularly intellectual, and have a short attention span for complex tasks that do not involve factional politics. Thus, Regan was not particularly enamored with his studies nor did he excel at them, although he later demonstrated that he had a practical genius for finance. Johnson initially resisted going to college and was more interested in campus politics while there than in his formal studies.

Street fighters, especially those not particularly gifted beyond their street savvy, eventually neglect the work of the organization and their own skills. They become so involved in strategies, negotiations, meetings, and attack that they let the organization's work slide, especially after they have held a leadership position for awhile and become bored.

Street fighters have a "shoot from the hip" philosophy. This applies to promises and proposed projects, as well as to factional conflicts. Street fighters are so unconcerned about details, and fall so behind in technical skills, that they frequently have little concept of what it takes to implement proposed projects. Thus, they over-commit, making promises that cannot be met. Disagreement in the organization over these promises as well as how to handle the inability to meet commitments begins the process of organizational decline.

Street fighters care more about reaching a decision, and much less about how that decision is implemented programmatically. Yet in the typical organization, implementation development and oversight is a key part of leadership. It is these tasks in particular that street fighters neglect. They exhibit little follow-through, fight hard to assure decision outcomes are favorable to their positions, and then devote little attention to making sure that even favorable decision outcomes are implemented.

Eventually, many street fighters meet their match by running into another, more skilled street fighter who wins the ensuing gang war. Sometimes street fighters who are lower in the organization are removed by top management when their divisions become such hotbeds of conflict and dissent that they become an embarrassment to the organization. But no street fighter goes softly into the night. They relinquish power, as they often govern, poorly. Those who have lost power are a sorry sight. Those with nowhere else to go may lurk around their organization, debilitated and demoralized. And frequently street fighters have nowhere else to go. The reputation for the infighting they generated by mismanagement and toxic leadership precedes them and closes doors. Some street fighters, rather than face the ignominy of constant contact with those over whom they once ruled, just slink away.

Protecting Yourself Against a Street Fighter

Street fighters are formidable allies and even more formidable foes. Here are some strategies for dealing with them in your organization.

Remember that street fighters see all relationships through the black-and-white lens of either being for or against them. Street fighters see few shades of gray, dividing the world into those who are for them and those who are against them. Do not inadvertently and without malice of forethought give the street fighter cause to place you in the latter camp, unless you clearly wish to be there.

Street fighters have a benevolent as well as a brutal side. Their sense of inadequacy does not make them need to hurt people. Rather it makes them need to dominate others. Their dominance may be benevolent at times as well as malevolent at others, and they may, unlike some other toxic leader types, freely distribute largess. First, doing so benefits team and gang member morale, causing the supporters of the street fighter to coalesce into a more fit fighting unit if need be. Second, distributing largess gives the street fighter a sense of power and dominance. As long as the street fighter with whom you interact is in such a benevolent mood, you might as well position yourself to be a beneficiary.

Most street fighters need people with organizational and technical skills, since they are inherently more interested in fighting the good fight than in routine and maintenance of the organization. Street fighters are motivators, speechmakers, and adrenalin pumpers. They are not exacting and dedicated paper pushers. Their organizations eventually drift awash in detail, neglecting paperwork, administrative (but not political) deadlines, and reports. If you offer these skills to a street fighter, you have earned a chit that can be called in later.

Link any plan or proposal you make to how it will benefit the street fighter and his organizational gang. If and when you make proposals, be sure to lay out how the plan enhances the welfare of the street fighter and his unit. Street fighters instinctively view every new idea from this angle. Smart street fighters will assess a plan's potential for protecting and expanding organizational turf immediately, but informally making the argument that your proposal is beneficial in this regard does not hurt.

The most endearing thing you can do for a street fighter is to promote his image of strength and dominance. Street fighters are keen image makers, aware of the importance that image and impression can wield. Thus, Johnson shrouded himself in the cloak of the cowboy and rancher. Wallace projected an image as a fighter against big institutions. Jackson formulated an image as the heir designate of civil rights leadership. Regan created an image as a no-nonsense chief of staff. Street fighters revel in, need, and demand such image-making. If a street fighter views you as helpful in this endeavor, you will be cherished, indeed.

If you decide to challenge a street fighter, be prepared for the brawl of your life. Street fighters, unlike bullies, are not intrinsic cowards. Unlike bullies, when faced with a tough situation, they will not cut and run. They do not pick out opponents who are inherently weaker, nor are they afraid of getting hurt in a fight. They are more afraid of losing than of getting hurt. So if you challenge a street fighter, you, too, should be ready to receive as well as inflict pain.

NOTES

1. Marshall Frady, *Wallace* (New York: The World, 1968), pp. 20–21.

2. Gail Sheehy, "Jesse Jackson: The Power or the Glory?" in *Character: America's Search for Leadership* (New York: William Morrow, 1988), pp. 78–123, esp. pp. 79–80.

3. Robert Dallek, *Lone Star Rising: Lyndon Johnson and His Times: 1908–1960* (New York: Oxford University Press, 1991), p. 476.

4. Ibid., p. 326.

5. Lou Cannon, *President Reagan: The Role of a Lifetime* (New York: Simon and Schuster, 1991), pp. 561–563.

6. George C. Wallace, *Stand Up for America* (Garden City, NY: Doubleday, 1976), pp. 70–107.

7. Ibid., pp. 63–64.

8. Ibid., p. 69.

9. Jody Carlson, *George C. Wallace and the Politics of Powerlessness: The Wallace Campaigns for the Presidency, 1964–1976* (New Brunswick, NJ: Transaction Books, 1981), p. 6.

10. Ibid., pp. 22–23.

11. Ibid., pp. 24–26.

12. Sheehy, pp. 94–95.

13. Ibid., pp. 96–97.

14. Ibid., pp. 88–90.

15. Ibid., pp. 108–112.

16. Ibid., p. 112.

17. Robert A. Caro, *The Path to Power: The Years of Lyndon Johnson* (New York: Alfred A. Knopf, 1982), p. 390.

18. Ronnie Dugger, *The Politician: The Life and Times of Lyndon Johnson—The Drive for Power, from the Frontier to Master of the Senate* (New York: W.W. Norton, 1982), pp. 325–339.

19. Robert A. Caro, *Means of Ascent: The Years of Lyndon Johnson* (New York: Alfred A. Knopf, 1990), pp. xxviii–xxix.

20. John P. Burke and Fred I. Greenstein, with Larry Berman and Richard Immerman, *How Presidents Test Reality: Decisions on Vietnam, 1954 and 1965* (New York: Russell Sage Foundation, 1989), p. 240.

21. Doris Kearns, *Lyndon Johnson and the American Dream* (New York: Harper and Row, 1976), pp. 262–263.

22. Ibid., p. 263.

23. Cannon, p. 567.

24. Ronald Reagan, *An American Life* (New York: Simon and Schuster, 1990), pp. 536–537.

25. Donald T. Regan, *For the Record: From Wall Street to Washington* (San Diego, CA: Harcourt Brace Jovanovich, 1988), pp. 359–377.

11

The Bully

Thumbnail Sketch of the Bully (Command Leadership Style): Bullies are very angry, pugnacious, command-style toxic leaders who are mad at the world and jealous of others who outperform them. They are driven to invalidate and tear others down in any setting, including and especially work. Bullies are bitter about past failures and denigrate others to feel less like failures themselves. Bullies control through a variety of means, including and especially inappropriate, angry, personalized outbursts that lash out with the force of an emotional tidal wave.

HALLMARK CHARACTERISTICS OF THE BULLY

The bully has several hallmark characteristics, but foremost among them, and encompassing many of the other characteristics, is the need to put other people down. Bullies need to invalidate others to feel good about themselves. The toxic organizational leader who is a bully, like the playground bully of yesteryear, wants to kick someone who is down. The most malicious of all the toxic leader types, the bully has a need to invalidate and even hurt others. Whereas for other toxic leader types, hurting others is not the primary drive but may be an unfortunate artifact of the toxic leader's approach to conducting business, for the bully, hurting others is a main goal. Bullies like to break fingers and draw blood, even if it is emotional rather than physical.

Of course, bullies do not admit that their primary goal is to tear others down, even to themselves. Bullies justify their behavior in organizational terms. They say they are attacking coworkers and colleagues for the benefit of the organization. Like street fighters, bullies sometimes develop a gang mentality among supporters, which is necessary to create an atmosphere where invalidating coworkers, rather than uplifting activities and productive work, are the goals.

Several prominent bullies show how this type of toxic leader likes to tear others down. J. Edgar Hoover was appointed director of the Federal Bureau of Investigation (FBI) in 1924, remaining in that office until his death in May 1972. The list of targets for Hoover's FBI was lengthy—liberals, communists, civil rights workers, and war protestors.[1] Raised in segregated Washington when his family's decreased financial fortunes meant that they could only sporadically hire hourly black help rather than have full time servants like "proper white folks," Hoover's attempt to smear and tear down Martin Luther King resembled a vendetta.[2] His tactics ranged from illegal wiretaps on the King home to heated public attacks.

Once Hoover determined that a journalist did not appreciate the Bureau sufficiently and therefore was an enemy, he would stop at nothing to destroy the journalist. He called unappreciative reporters "journalistic prostitutes." In public, Hoover maintained minimal decorum with Drew Pearson, a prominent columnist. In private, however, Hoover maintained a four-thousand-page file on Pearson. The FBI director scribbled into that file that Pearson was a "whelp," who "still continues his regurgitation." Hoover called Pearson a "jackal" who indulged in "psychopathic lyings."[3] James Wechsler, *New York Post* editor, was a "rat." Walter Lippman was a "coyote of the press." Tom Wicker of the *New York Times* was a "jerk" with "mental halitosis." Art Buchwald was a "sick alleged humorist." With no evidence or proof, Hoover reported to the White House that columnist Joseph Alsop was a homosexual and *Los Angeles Times* reporter Jack Nelson was a drunk.[4] For the first thirty-five years of his Bureau directorship, his tactics succeeded in bullying every major publication but the *New Yorker* from seriously reporting anything on the bureau beyond FBI press releases.

Joseph McCarthy, a Republican U.S. senator from Wisconsin, represented bullyhood incarnate in addition to his state. One biographer refers to his persona as that of a "buccaneer" and a "pirate," calling McCarthy's unfulfilled presidential ambitions as "moral leprosy."[5] Rising to power on the Cold War swell of anti-communism, McCarthy was elected to the Senate in 1946.[6] He remained there until his death from alcoholism at age forty-eight in 1957.[7] Until his censure by the Senate in December of 1954, McCarthy used his position as chairman of the Permanent Investigations Subcommittee of the Senate Committee on Government Operations to purge thousands of government employees, educators, labor leaders, journalists, scientists, writers, and entertainers, as well as to intimidate hundreds of thousands more.[8]

Another bully was Jim Jones, leader of the San Francisco based religious cult the People's Temple. Jones, a "petty tyrant" and "false prophet," was filled with hatred and bitterness that he used to "dehumanize, brutalize," and "tyrannize his following."[9] In his ministry, Jones announced that all people who participated in racism, sexism, and contributed to poverty were subhuman, and therefore nonpersons. He preached that the rest of society had a plan to destroy every black person in America.[10] In the end, it was Jones himself who ordered the destruction and untimely deaths of over nine hundred of his followers in the South American jungles of Guyana in 1978.[11]

Jones was accused of bullying followers into turning over their belongings to him, taking the wives of close subordinates, and even forcing followers to sign blank papers and false confessions of heinous crimes, such as child abuse, to be used as the church saw fit. He was suspected of murdering those who defected, and ultimately did order the murder of Congressman Leo Ryan and others in his delegation who went to Jonestown, Guyana to investigate reports of abuse. Fearing the retribution that would occur, Jones ordered his entire flock of over nine hundred to drink cyanide laced Kool-Aid. They did, along with him and the entire Temple hierarchy, and died.[12]

Former President Richard Nixon had many characteristics that veered toward being a bully. In his first race for Congress, Nixon displayed the personalized negative political tactics that he would use throughout his career.[13] Winning a California congressional seat in a 1946 race with Democratic opponent Jerry Voorhis, Nixon managed to suggest that Voorhis was a communist supporter or a dupe. He told journalist Stewart Alsop that "then there are the Don Quixotes, who never accomplish anything, the idealistic men—like Jerry Voorhis."[14]

Tom Wicker describes Nixon as dividing the world into the "haves" and the "have nots," placing himself in the latter category. Nixon, when encountering someone he perceived to be in the "have" category, became instinctively hostile and set out to attack the privileged. He defined most of his political opponents this way. Once in Congress, this driving hostility contributed to his carefully orchestrated hearings while on the House Un-American Activities Committee that destroyed Alger Hiss.[15] During Vietnam, he became paranoid and developed enemies lists which were used by the White House to keep track of and harass those in opposition to administration policies.[16] The Watergate tactics and dirty tricks that flourished during his administration are also those of a bully. In August 1974, Nixon resigned the presidency under threat of impeachment for his role in the Watergate affair.

Bullies take themselves very seriously. More than any other type, they engage in bragging and exaggerate their exploits and contributions to the organization. Jones told his congregation that he was a "dynamo," a "hydraulic system," and that Christ was using his body. Jones had a well-known, prodigious, sexual appetite for both men and women, and was praised by one associate who wrote, "I admire you greatly to be able to fuck anyone for the cause." Jones would brag about one occasion when he had sex with sixteen people in one day.[17]

Yet Jones was not a hedonist in the sense of using sex for pleasure. His power needs and bullying tactics dominated his concern. He used sex to tie people to the group and as a club to punish and humiliate. Jones promoted himself as the ultimate sex object, dispensing favors to an adoring following. He used his body to assert superiority and to humiliate, and discovered "the reputation destroying power of sexual rumors and innuendo."[18] He seesawed between promiscuity and celibacy, bullying his followers into accepting his mood of the moment.

Jones denounced conventional sexual mores and jealousies as egotistical and hypocritical, and adopted a doctrine that he was the only true heterosexual. He made church members stand up and publicly admit homosexual feelings or acts. He forced planning commission members for the Temple to list all the sexual partners, male and female, in their life, as well as the type of sex. He coerced wives into standing up and complaining publicly about their husbands' lovemaking. He had sex with some men in the church, ostensibly to prove to them their homosexuality, as well as with many women.

The climate Jones created was one of intolerance, guilt, and repression, under the guise of tolerance, so that any member could censure any other member for "selfish" sexual behavior, labeling each other as "homosexual," "queer," "lesbian," "male chauvinist pig," "sexist," and "narcisstic." Any behavior perceived as homosexual was punished. But heterosexual behavior was condemned as compensating for homosexual feelings, and also punished, sometimes by Jones sodomizing the members he contended harbored such feelings to punish them.[19] Sometimes he linked his "savior" qualities to sex and used it to "save" rebellious or suicidal Temple women.

After largely ignoring gangsters during the crime ridden 1920s, beginning in the 1930s, Hoover excelled at promoting a favorable image of the FBI as a crime fighting agency and a positive view of his own contributions to it. He became absorbed with public relations and opinion making. A series of glamorizing articles showing the FBI as clean-cut men combatting the evils of crime began to appear under his signature in *American Magazine*. Appearing between February 1934 and August 1936, the articles carried such titles as "Gun Crazy" and were written by Hoover's ghost writer, Courtney Ryley Cooper, a former *Denver Post* staff writer. Cooper was added to the Justice Department payroll to help Henry Suydam, a former Washington correspondent for *Brooklyn Eagle*, carry out a public relations program for the bureau. Cooper wrote an introduction for Hoover's first book glamorizing the bureau, *Persons in Hiding*, and Hoover wrote an introduction for Cooper's book doing the same, *Ten Thousand Public Enemies.*

When the gangster of the era, John Dillinger, was gunned down by fifteen bureau agents outside of Chicago's Biograph movie theater, Hoover hung up Dillinger's picture "like a scalp" in bureau offices all over the country, and posed for newspapers with Dillinger's hat, gun, and "perhaps an ear."[20] Hoover granted privileged access to his personal friend and newspaper reporter, Rex Collier, for his syndicated column, "War on Crime," which was, in theory part of a national education campaign to stamp out crime in the United States, but in reality was part of a national public relations campaign to promote Hoover's and the bureau's image.

A 1937 Brookings Institution study noted that with the creation of the FBI National Police Academy, the adoption of the FBI as a clearing house for information on criminals, bureau organization of state and local conferences, and Hoover's remarkably successful propaganda campaign, the bureau acquired an image of being armed, trained, mobile, fearlessly in pursuit of criminals, and invincible. When, later, Hoover was ordered by the Justice Department to curtail his public relations campaign, the bureau resisted and maintained a high profile, and added a new concern—dissidents and internal security issues. Subsequently, O'Reilly reports that "FBI bureaucrats soon became more interested in public and congressional attitudes toward dissidents and internal security policy than gangsters and crime control."[21]

Senator McCarthy was also prone to self-promotion and hyperbole. He portrayed himself as a defender of democracy and freedom, contending that "the ends he strives for is the ending of the Communist infiltration and subversion that would destroy democracy in the United States."[22] Elected a judge in Wisconsin three years out of law school at age thirty-three, McCarthy later resigned to join the Marines during World War II. Although he had previously written the recruiting officer to ask for a commission, he duped the *Milwaukee Journal* into writing a story about how the judge was so eager to serve he was willing to join as a private or anything else, in a burst of patriotism.[23] McCarthy used the war and his uniform to gain maximum political advantage by building up a myth of himself as red-blooded and patriotic, willing to compete with eighteen- and nineteen-year-old men to see if he was worthy of a commission. Nor did he resign his judgeship, but persuaded other judges to take over his caseload while he was gone, thereby exhibiting their patriotism as well, but working a hardship on the Wisconsin courts.

Bullies are arrogant and appear self-assured. Close inspection of their actual productivity, however, reveals that for many, their bragging has little or no basis in actual performance. Fearful that other employees will notice how lazy most bullies actually are, bullies are incredibly jealous of those more successful than themselves. Sometimes their activities do little to enhance organizational output and everything to enhance the image of the bully. The FBI, for example, did not become a major crime fighter throughout the twenties and into the thirties. Later, under Hoover's direction, it chased dissidents and protestors instead of organized crime, a sticky wicket Hoover refused initially to tackle.

Hoover biographer Anthony Summers was later to charge that this denial of the Mafia at the time it was making its ascent was due to the Mafia blackmailing Hoover over his private life. Hoover had an unexplained relationship with Mafia godfather Frank Costello his whole life, claiming to have met Costello window shopping on Fifth Avenue. Hoover also knew "Lucky" Luciano and Meyer Lansky, frequenting the same watering holes in Florida that Lansky did. There was no federal effort to prosecute Lansky until after two years after Hoover died, and then prosecution was initiated by the Internal Revenue Service, not the FBI. Summers contends that the mob had hard evidence that Hoover was homosexual and used it to neutralize FBI actions against their operations.[24]

Unlike street fighters who do enjoy seeing other employees succeed under circumstances that reflect positively on their own leadership, bullies become very jealous of the accomplishments of others and do not enjoy seeing others succeed. Hoover, for example, never liked Melvin Purvis, the agent in charge of the FBI team that gunned down John Dillinger. He was jealous of the attention Purvis attracted and disapproved of the fact that Purvis wrote a book. According to Ugo Carusi, an executive assistant to six different attorney generals, Hoover, the titular author of several promoting books himself "always looked askance at agents who wrote books."[25] Indeed, Purvis is not even mentioned in Hoover's book.

Hoover was also jealous of the role Treasury agents played, particularly in the Lindbergh case, and of one Treasury official in particular, Elmer Irey, labeled by some subordinates as "the greatest cop of all time." According to Malachi Harney, an agent serving under Hoover, Hoover and Irey were bitter enemies, in part because Irey was critical of the FBI's civil service investigations for Treasury personnel.[26] Later, Hoover, who turned down a scholarship to the University of Virginia because he "couldn't afford it," and never moved out of the house his mother lived in until she died nor away from the District of Columbia where he was born and raised, became jealous of "those arrogant Harvard-type Kennedy men."[27]

Bullies, then, differ from street fighters in their response to other more energetic, more talented, harder working employees. Street fighters will not be threatened, per se, will encourage the employee to continue to be productive, and then will try to take credit for the employee's success and hard work.

A street fighter will argue that the success would not have been possible without his own magnanimous leadership. The bully will try to destroy the employee, or at the very least, create such a difficult environment that continued high productivity is impossible.

The hallmark emotion of bullies is anger. They are angry at everything. Frequently, they appear to be caustic and bitter, having learned to tone down their anger into slightly more socially acceptable forms. Bullies have always been angry, even when young, but across time, their anger and tendencies toward bullying others have grown, especially if not checked or curbed within the workplace. Their cleverness at concealing the unacceptable aspects of their bullying behavior has also grown across the years, so watch out for aging bullies with power! Nothing appears more fearsome than bullies backed into a corner where they perceive their credibility on the line and their position in the organization at stake. In such instances, bullies will lash out with a tidal wave of emotion, totally inappropriate and unexpected, that overwhelms critics and opponents who are not prepared for such irrational response. Nixon's public outbursts are legendary, including his tirade in 1962 after losing the race for California governor that the press would no longer have him to kick around.

Hoover would indulge public outbursts against smut, peddlers of filth, and sexual perversions. Hoover himself, however, was a closet homosexual who was in the constant company of his lover and assistant FBI director, Clyde Tolson, especially after his mother's death. He never formulated or had a substantial relationship with a woman other than his mother, remaining deeply ambivalent toward women his entire life.[28] Hoover promoted Tolson from new agent to assistant director in three years, with no field experience. Despite Hoover's private behavior, he never acknowledged his homosexuality publicly, and in fact, would engage in public diatribes against pornography and homosexuality. He ordered his agents to infiltrate homosexual rights groups across the country, to collect names of members and take photographs to determine if the groups were subversive. After twenty-three years of such activity, the FBI finally concluded that the activists were not subversive.[29]

Like playground bullies, toxic leader bullies are always perceiving slights when none are intended. Criticized bullies will imply that their reputations have been irreparably damaged, and will demand immediate and public apologies for normal routine organizational actions. They perceive themselves to be backed into corners when concerns about their problem areas are raised, and when trustworthy leaders and even less malicious toxic leaders would consider the substance of the criticisms as legitimate issues of debate. Bullies so readily perceive slights and corners because their real need is to find a target on which to release their incredibly staggering anger, so even the slightest or most legitimate issue if linked at all to their own behavior will do. Some bullies become paranoid, seeing enemies everywhere. The tendency to see imagined enemies they loathe helps create the real enemies they fear.

Bullies love to claim that they are legal experts, and use their presumed knowledge of the law and of organizational rules like a club to beat other employees into submission. They frequently threaten lawsuits against co-workers, a favorite bully tactic. They leave the grounds for any charges vaguely defined and unspecified, because typically there aren't any. Bullies will also threaten to fire or get fired offending employees, even when no documenta-tion or steps have been taken toward this end, when no grounds for such actions exist, and when no support for it exists at higher levels within the organization.

Hoover, a man of many prejudices, including discrimination against blacks, women, and Jews, used the bully technique of threatening to fire people and on occasion, did so.[30] William Sullivan, former assistant to the director, reports that Hoover used dismissal with prejudice frequently, even though doing so made it almost impossible for the discharged person to get another job, particularly in the government. A widely cited bureau black joke goes that one day Tolson went in to see Hoover to report that he was feeling depressed and melancholy and was thinking of going home and going to bed. The joke's punchline is Hoover's response. Hoover urges Tolson not to go home in order to feel better, but to just go down the list, pick someone and go out and fire him. Tolson, apparently when told he can do so "with prejudice"—the equivalent of a dishonorable discharge from the military—leaves the office beaming.[31]

Even if bullies have no intention of following through on threats, and if they know the threats are hollow, they enjoy the emotional distress they create in their targets and victims. Thus they watch in enjoyment for any indication of weakness in their victims and targets. Signs of weakness in victims excite bullies and cause them to continue, augment, and expand their bullying tactics and activities. An inveterate miser, Hoover used his power to bully gifts out of agents and everyone else, and died a millionaire. Former assistant director Sullivan reports: "Hoover was always hitting on us for gifts, and we'd have to buy him extremely expensive gifts." The occasions on which gifts were expected included his anniversary with the Justice Department, his anniversary with the bureau, Thanksgiving Day, Christmas Day, and numer-ous other occasions. The request would come from Tolson, but agents knew that Tolson and Hoover were keeping tabs on whether the total matched the recommended contributions per agent. Hoover used bureau employees to write *Masters of Deceit*, a bestseller published under his name by Henry Holt and Co., and personally pocketed all the royalties. He had sweetheart deals with some rich businessmen, including Clint Murchison, who owned the publishing company, whereby Hoover would invest a small amount and share in any accrued profits but not in any losses.[32]

In addition to using his power to gain gifts and other favors, Hoover used the information his agency collected to retain his position in the bureau, despite the fact that several presidents would have preferred to replace him. Sullivan related that Hoover had information for years and years on people in high ranking positions—all the irregularities and embarrassing incidents in their lives, including but not limited to sexual peccadillos. Hoover also collected information on financial improprieties and political chicanery, and then implied what he knew to the person about whom he had incriminating evidence, "convincing" them to see his point of view. Hoover's bully club was the most damaging kind of knowledge—knowledge of people's misbehavior.[33] Hoover shrewdly softened and balanced his threats by entertaining high officials with bureau money and providing information selectively to solidify his support.

Bullies engage in threats of all sorts so much that even they are not sure when they are bluffing and when they really mean it. Threats are a way of life for the bully. In fits of anger, the more aggressive ones will foolishly threaten superiors as well as more dependent and easily cowed subordinates. Bullies typically threaten superiors and equals, however, only when their own position is secure, for conscious risk-taking is not in the bully behavioral repertoire. In fact, bullies abhor risks, which is why they lash out so viciously at perceived threats—both real and imagined—with counterthreats. Any threat to a bully constitutes an unacceptable risk.

Behind all the threats, counterthreats, belligerence, and bellicosity, bullies harbor a secret: just like playground bullies, toxic leader bullies are cowards. Unlike street fighters, who relish taking on competing factions under any circumstances, including fair play, bullies abhor a level playing ground, as much as or more than they abhor risks. In fact, bullies abhor a level playing ground because such conditions entail risks—the risks that others will outperform them, and the risks that the logic and arguments of others will prevail. Bullies work to create an emotionally charged atmosphere of threats and fear where their own emotional outbursts work to maximum advantage, intuitively sensing that in a more rational, healthy environment, their outbursts will be viewed as the inappropriate tactics they are.

Because bullies are secret cowards despite all their anger and aggressiveness, when challenged vigorously, their bluffs become apparent. When confronted with major challenges, they will back down to lick their wounds. But bullies do not forgive and forget. They will lay in wait for days, months, and years to extract revenge from those who have wronged them. Indeed, waiting for revenge is one of the few instances when bullies, normally an impetuous, angry sort, exhibit patience.

Likely Sources of Sense of Inadequacy for the Bully

Bullies are not self-revealing, unlike street fighters who will pal around as buddies, so the source of their anger may be deeply hidden. More likely it is many sources, but all of the sources can be traced back to a massive sense of personal failure. The source of the sense of inadequacy of other toxic leaders is much more likely to be traced back to system problems, childhood family circumstances, or factors beyond the toxic leader's control. For example, the sense of shame in the case of absentee leaders may be rooted in the social class of the childhood family. The small man syndrome—both physical and emotional varieties—of scrappy street fighters is rooted in biological genes or childhood family circumstances also beyond the toxic leader's control.

In contrast to these other toxic leaders, the driving sense of inadequacy for the bully is far more personal. The bully feels he has, and, indeed, frequently really has failed in the past. Only occasionally, the failure may not be actually the fault of the youthful bully, or even a failure at all, but the child lacks the ability to distinguish and internalizes the failure as personal. Mostly, bullies have failed at some key endeavor earlier in their lives. Rather than respond to failure, real or perceived, with a determination to learn from it and overcome it, the bully becomes very angry and bitter, blaming the system and others for failures that were really within the bully's personal control. The more angry and malicious the bully, the longer the string of previous failures for which the bully may legitimately be held personally accountable, but for which the bully refuses to accept any personal responsibility.

Nixon's sense of failure may have resulted from considerable sibling rivalry, and then his mother leaving him behind twice, to care for a brother ailing from tuberculosis in the dry climate of Arizona. The brother died, contributing to Nixon's guilt. Nixon's father, Frank, was also insecure, had a temper, and by reports, was somewhat of a bully himself, generating fear in his son. Frank did not allow any challenges from his children, and deprived them of learning confidence through mastering and dominating.[34] The conflict within Nixon between the more pacifist nature from his mother and the more belligerent, insecure nature from his father would be suppressed for periods but then released in explosions. Nixon also, as the Watergate tapes reveal and friends already knew, used profanity quite freely.

The likely source of Hoover's bullying was his psychological inability to accept and deal with his own sexuality and the constant paranoia that he would be discovered. This conflict drove Hoover to seek medical help in 1946 from a psychiatrist. He went to the diagnostic clinic of Clark, King, and Carter, which handled many well-known patients, and was soon referred to Dr. Marshall de G. Ruffin, becoming a life-long patient of Ruffin.[35] While homosexuality today is likely to be viewed as genetic, that is not a view Hoover would have readily embraced, holding himself to blame.

Jim Jones was born to a semi-invalid father injured by mustard gas in World War I and an ambitious mother who worked a depressing job in a factory. In his Indiana town where many residents were of German descent, Jones looked dark and almost Asian, later claiming he had some Indian blood. Jones was ashamed of his family and their lack of normality, and perhaps of his role in it, since his mother worked at a poorly paid job to earn money for his college education. By age four, he was swearing profanities as entertainment before town men to earn money for sodas. According to Reiterman, Jones internalized the shame and pain of being alone most of the time and an outcast, reporting later:

> I was ready to kill by the end of the third grade. I mean, I was so fucking aggressive and hostile, I was ready to kill. Nobody gave me any love, any understanding. In those days a parent was supposed to go with a child to school functions. . . . There was some kind of school performance, and everybody's fucking parent was there but mine. I'm standing there. Alone. Always was alone.[36]

In high school, he did almost kill his best friend, shooting at the friend with his father's pistol for leaving after dinner when Jones did not want to be left alone.

Often, the favored tactics of bullies provide insight into their previous personal failures, with tactics employed that reveal the area in which the bully is most insecure. Bullies that frequently threaten to launch law suits against others may have gone to but not successfully completed law school, either flunking or dropping out prior to graduation. Bullies that charge others with acting unethically and unprofessionally may be acutely aware of the lack of ethics in their own behavior. Bullies that threaten to fire others may have on an earlier occasion been fired themselves, sometimes more than once. University professors who become bullies may have been denied tenure elsewhere, leaving them bitter and angry. Public officials who become bullies may have been moved to unpleasant trivial jobs under the guise of reorganization. Corporate officials and consultants may have just been fired outright.

The deep sense of personal failure that all bullies share is underpinned by an even deeper fear of further failure. Initially, this fear of failure paralyzed bullies in their attempt to perform and meet organizational productivity standards and norms. Unlike the street fighter that would rather do something, even if it is wrong, than be subjected to inaction, in the mind of the bully paralyzed by fear of failure, it is better to do nothing at all than to do something that is wrong and fail. Thus begins a pattern of nonproductivity and failure to perform, whereby the bully engages in behavior that assures the very thing he most fears.

Eventually, the fear of failure becomes a convenient cover for a general and intellectual laziness that also characterizes most bullies. Laziness is un-American and antithetical to organizational success. U.S. culture, incredibly forgiving, will accommodate lack of intelligence, lack of money, lack of social standing, and lack of many things before it will accommodate lack of the work ethic. A cognitive dissonance develops between what bullies recognize unconsciously if not consciously is a criterion for success and their own behavior.

The public image of bullies as hard working is often belied by the private facts. Even as a child, Jim Jones did not like to get dirty, and as an adult, left the work of the Temple to members who did his bidding. Hoover, despite his hard working public image, liked gambling, the races, jai alai, and good food. He never missed a lunch or dinner with Tolson in about forty years, and had two limousines following him everywhere, in case one should break down. He refused to walk even short distances, drive himself, or take public transportation. Every night he began dinner with six mini-bottles at the same Washington restaurant, and by today's standard would be called an alcoholic. Joe McCarthy drank heavily, to the point where, especially at the end, it interfered with his work. He died of alcoholism at age forty-eight.

Unconscious if not conscious knowledge of this and the cognitive dissonance it provokes makes the bully even angrier and contrasts unfavorably with other toxic leader types, all of whom work at something. The street fighter works very hard at maintaining his faction and organizational gang battles. The enforcer works hard at whatever the leading toxic leader wants. The busybody works hard at holding rumor court. The controller works very hard in undifferentiated fashion at about everything. Even the absentee leader works hard at symbolic manipulation and myth creation on his brief stints in the organization. The only thing at which the bully works hard is revenge and even those spells of activity do not last much longer than his inappropriate emotional outbursts.

Bullies are not limited by normal moral boundaries. Unlike absentee leaders, busybodies, and controllers, bullies will knowingly engage in unethical behaviors that border on or cross over into malfeasance. Despite their lip service to the importance of the law, they will hide, manipulate, and manufacture evidence if they need to do so to get at a target. They will manipulate

and manufacture personnel records, placing great emphasis upon the personnel file as a substitute for more concrete measures of productivity and
performance and regard placing negative letters and memos in the personnel
files of targeted employees as great personal victories. Hoover violated the
law, not only in his sweetheart investments and acceptance of gratuities but
in releasing public information for private purposes and collecting information illegally. McCarthy similarly played fast and loose with legalities in his
red-baiting investigations. Jones left the country with his flock, in part, to get
away from the reaches of U.S. law.

Needless to say, bullies operate almost exclusively at Maslow's level two.
Their fears and sense of inadequacy cause them to be continuously concerned
about safety, seeing threats to their personal safety where none exist. In order
to justify their own nonproductivity, bullies see enemies everywhere. Bullies
need enemies onto whom they can project their deep anger. Their anger is
so deep and their moral character has become so flabby that to turn it inward
would be devastating. Even if turning their anger inward did not destroy
themselves, doing so would blow their convenient cover for laziness and
would require them to actually engage in productive work. Many bullies,
particularly aging ones, have not engaged in intellectually productive work
for years and have forgotten how to do it, if they ever knew.

BULLIES AND THE ORGANIZATION

Operational Style and Tactics of the Bully

Whatever the initial specific sources of the sense of personal failure bullies
have, the impact has been compounded subsequently by the bully's own
behavior. As bullies strike out at others, their behavior evokes hostile responses from those attacked who legitimately try to defend themselves. Bullies
then respond to the defense others put forth with even more malicious attacks.
With each successive round of threat and charges from the bully, followed
by defensive maneuvers from those attacked, the bully's response grows more
disproportionate to any stimuli. Before long, they reach paranoia and perceive
enemies everywhere, creating an emotionally charged, dysfunctional organizational environment in the process.

The tactics of the bully may at times seem to resemble those of the street
fighter when the latter is in the throes of a heated battle with an opposing
faction. But such appearances, like much about the bully, are deceptive. The
tactics and mindset of the bully are far more personal than those of the street
fighter. The street fighter usually manages to depersonalize actions and
responses within the organization enough to think in terms of battle tactics

if not strategy. The street fighter recognizes that other people have some motivations and incentives that are intrinsic to themselves and independent of the street fighter. The bully does not. The bully personalizes the actions of all other organizational actors to one degree or another. Even when the bully recognizes that other employees have intrinsic drives that cause them to act in certain ways, the bully still takes these actions as a personal affront.

The bully can exhibit considerable bursts of energy when first given a new position from which the bully can puff, brag, and exert petty authority blended with maliciousness. The first actions of one bully, for example, upon acquiring a new position on merely an acting basis, were to immediately take over the most spacious, previously shared office space when all other professionals and staff were in cramped quarters, to move the xerox machine to an inaccessible area, to deny access to mails for most organizational business, to deny supplies to any professional for any purpose including the basic organizational mission, and to request to superiors in writing that several subordinates be fired immediately.

Such tactics constituted an interesting mix of pettiness and malice and were of course justified as being in the well-being of the organization. Their impact was to inhibit productivity and undercut organizational health. Such bursts of activity are not typically sustained, however, but occur only when the bully has suddenly acquired new power and is still amused with its novelty. Typically the bully quickly becomes bored, for effective use of real power requires real work. Activity bursts also occur when the bully is backed in to a corner.

Impact of the Bully on the Organization

As the most malicious type of toxic leader, bullies have a devastating impact on their organizations. The intensity of their anger and the inappropriateness of their tactics exceed those of any other toxic leader. The main factor that keeps bullies from destroying the organizations they govern is that their tenure tends to be short. They lack the charisma of the street fighter to build and sustain supportive governing factions. Their emotional outbursts are eventually turned on too many people. Even those employees who have not personally experienced the wrath of the bully become suspicious and less supportive, realizing from observing how others have been treated how arbitrary and vindictive the bully can be.

For periods of short duration, bullies can become the organizational pied pipers, leading employees and subordinates in directions counter to their fundamental interests. But the tendency of bullies to personalize all actions, coupled with their laziness, assures that the bully's pied piper period will be limited. Bullies who manage to attract and keep the loyalty of capable enforcers will survive longer than bullies who do not. But the extreme jealousy bullies exhibit toward anyone even remotely successful usually means that they are only able to attract support staff dependent upon the bully for their jobs, or untalented enforcers. Talented enforcers will eventually be bought by and shift loyalties to more stable, less belligerent, and less arbitrary toxic leaders. Or else, the bully will sooner or later turn on and destroy his own enforcers in reaction to some perceived slight. Nixon's most trusted foreign policy advisor, Henry Kissinger, was foreign born and constitutionally prohibited from running for the presidency should he have been so inclined, thus serving as no direct threat to Nixon's power.

Bullies, like enforcers, seldom become the top leader in an organization. Only in the rarest of circumstances do bullies move into top level leadership. They are promoted to power only when a leadership vacuum exists and few other alternatives are available, or when they aggressively seize it. More typically, they reside in lower levels of management, undercut in their upward mobility by their anger and laziness. But unlike street fighters who are driven to be king of the mountain, bullies do not care about being number one. They care most about attacking perceived threats in their immediate organizational environment and invalidating others, especially those more productive, in order to feel good.

In the long run, toxic leader bullies, like playground bullies, stand alone. They are unloved, uncherished, and not missed when they fall. Their bitterness and anger makes it difficult for even supporters to be around them for long periods of time and eventually, they are ignored by others, just as for years they have ignored productive work.

Protecting Yourself Against a Bully

Beware of the toxic leader bully! He can make your life just as miserable as the playground bully of years before. Here are things you should do.

Leave, leave, leave. The first rule of smart buying in real estate is "location, location, location." The same rule applies to dealing with toxic leader bullies. The further you are located from one, the better off you are. Or, translated into an action plan, when unexpectedly confronted with a toxic leader bully heading up your organization or unit, "leave, leave, leave." Even if initially you feel you have developed a method of accommodating the bully, bullies are irascible and unpredictable; the accommodation saps your energy and productivity, and ultimately, will fail if the bully perceives you as a threat, for appeasement only eggs them on. Leave while the leaving is good, even if it is difficult. Several followers of Jim Jones tried to leave his Temple once it was relocated to the South American jungles but he always urged them to stay another day, another week. Ultimately they ended up sharing another lifetime with him in death, which some of the few survivors report was not voluntary but coerced.

Do not forsake your principles. Bullies often bring down their own shame and ignominy on the organizations they lead. Several enforcers for Richard Nixon went to prison over their role in the Watergate affair. Jones's followers participated in rituals and confessions that made it difficult to integrate back into mainstream society, contributing to their following him into mass suicide. McCarthy's platform, the Un-American Activities Committee, was ultimately disbanded, and those who participated in the red hunt smeared with the association in later years when public opinion shifted. So giving up your principles, little by little, to appease the bully and to live in his world, not only leaves you without an ethical center. It is a dangerous route.

Showing weakness can be fatal. Some toxic leaders, such as the controller and the busybody, will respond to any complaints you have and weaknesses you exhibit with sympathy. But not the bully. When the bully sees weakness, he moves in to exploit it. The exploitation may not be immediate, but the weakness is now stored in the bully's mental weapons cabinet, to be used when needed, much like Hoover brought out incriminating information on others at times he felt threatened or that he needed to. Sometimes, as the episodes of Hoover firing people with no regard to the consequences for them indicate, bullies exploit weaknesses just "for the hell of it," that is, because they can. If you do not show vulnerability and weakness, it does not mean that the bully will change his ways, but it does mean that he will likely pick another target for his anger, for bullies have an internal, psychological radar that allows them to zero in on the weak link. Hopefully, it isn't you.

Know that most bullies can be beaten. Bullies, despite their ferociousness and larger-than-life images, are cowards. Despite dispensing hurts with abandon, bullies do not like to be hurt themselves. The blood that they like to see is not their own. They pick weak targets. If you indicate that you are not going to take abuse and stand up to the bully, sometimes they back down. Even when they do not, they can be beaten. Part of their powerfulness and image of invincibility comes from preventing such challenges, nipping organizational coups in the bud, for they instinctively know that they would lose if subjected to a well-planned all-out attack.

Look for the smoking gun. The ideal way to challenge a bully is with a smoking gun—the thing that bullies most fear to have revealed. For Hoover, it was his homosexuality—incriminating information in the social climate of the times used to "blackmail" him, just as he used incriminating information to politically extort others. For Nixon, it was his role in the Watergate affair and cover-up. For McCarthy, it was the fact that his patriotic red-hunting masked a personal meanness that, when exposed, turned the American people away. For Jones, it was the disappearance and probable murder of Temple members who tried to dissent and leave. The smoking gun will vary from bully to bully, but it is usually there if you search hard enough. The bully may go to great lengths, as did Hoover, to cover it up, but his own behavior—what he lashes out against most vehemently in public—may give you clues. Do some sleuth work and find this smoking gun if you can.

Go outside the organization for help. If you are being attacked by a bully toxic leader and are under siege, go outside your organization or unit for help. Others would no doubt also like to remove the bully from power. Those inside the organization may be too fearful to challenge the bully, but those outside may provide assistance. Turn to former employees, trustworthy leaders within other parts of the organization, stockholders, constituents, the press, and public opinion. All is fair in love and war, unless you are dealing with a bully, and then fairness isn't the issue. It is a case of organizational, psychological, emotional, and sometimes, as the case of Jim Jones shows, even physical life and death.

NOTES

1. Athan G. Theoharis and John Stuart Cox, *The Boss: J. Edgar Hoover and the Great American Inquisition* (Philadelphia: Temple University Press, 1988), pp. 14–15.

2. David J. Garrow, *The FBI and Martin Luther King, Jr.: From "Solo" to Memphis* (New York: W. W. Norton, 1981), pp. 101–150.

3. Anthony Summers, *Official and Confidential: The Secret Life of J. Edgar Hoover* (New York: G. P. Putnam's Sons, 1993), p. 100.

4. Ibid., p. 101.

5. Lately Thomas, *When Angels Wept: The Senator Joseph McCarthy Affair: A Story Without a Hero* (New York: William Morrow, 1973), pp. 7, 201, 226.

6. Jack Anderson and Ronald W. May, *McCarthy: The Man, the Senator, and the "Ism"* (Boston: Beacon Press, 1952), p. 114.

7. Roberta Strauss Feuerlicht, *Joe McCarthy and McCarthyism: The Hate that Haunts America* (New York: McGraw-Hill, 1972), pp. 146–149.

8. Robert Griffith, *The Politics of Fear: Joseph R. McCarthy and the Senate*, 2nd ed. (Amherst: University of Massachusetts Press, 1987), p. xix.

9. James Reston, Jr., *Our Father Who Art in Hell* (New York: Times Books, 1981), p. 58.

10. David Chidester, *Salvation and Suicide: An Interpretation of Jim Jones, the Peoples Temple, and Jonestown* (Bloomington: Indiana University Press, 1988), pp. 63–72.

11. Judith Mary Weightman, *Making Sense of the Jonestown Suicides* (New York: Edwin Mellen Press, 1983).

12. Tim Reiterman with John Jacobs, *Raven: The Untold Story of the Reverend Jim Jones and His People* (New York: E. P. Dutton, 1982), pp. 1–5.

13. Jerry Voorhis, *The Strange Case of Richard Milhous Nixon* (New York: Paul S. Eriksson, 1972), pp. 1–10.

14. Tom Wicker, *One of Us: Richard Nixon and the American Dream* (New York: Random House, 1991), pp. 46–47.

15. Ibid., pp. 59–70.

16. J. Anthony Lukas, *Nightmare: The Underside of the Nixon Years* (New York: Viking Press, 1976), pp. 12–13.

17. John R. Hall, *Gone from the Promised Land: Jonestown in American Cultural History* (New Brunswick, NJ: Transaction Books, 1987), pp. 112–113.

18. Reiterman, p. 172.

19. Ibid., p. 173.

20. Kenneth O'Reilly, *Hoover and the Un-Americans: The FBI, HUAC, and the Red Menace* (Philadelphia: Temple University Press, 1983), pp. 32–33.

21. Ibid., p. 34.

22. James Rorty and Moshe Decter, *McCarthy and the Communists* (Boston: Beacon Press, 1954), p. 51.

23. Anderson, p. 54.

24. Summers, pp. 237–254.

25. Ovid Demaris, *The Director: An Oral Biography of J. Edgar Hoover* (New York: Harper's Magazine Press, 1975), p. 58.

26. Ibid., pp. 61–63.

27. Ibid., pp. 252–253.

28. Summers, pp. 100–125.

29. Ibid., p. 93.

30. Ibid., pp. 54–80.

31. Demaris, p. 85.

32. Ibid., pp. 92–93.

33. Ibid., p. 96.

34. Eli S. Chesen, *President Nixon's Psychiatric Profile: A Psychodynamic-Genetic Interpretation* (New York: Peter H. Wyden, 1973), pp. 67–69.

35. Summers, pp. 94–95.

36. Reiterman, pp. 16–17.

V

TOXIC LEADERS AND
ORGANIZATIONAL CYCLES

12

Toxic Leaders and Organizational Decline

Trustworthy leadership is what we all want, but do not always get. Under trustworthy leadership, the mission of the organization is pursued collectively so that the combined resources of the people working in the organization are greater than the whole. Each employee brings various strengths to the workplace, as well as some weaknesses. Trustworthy leaders skillfully interface these various strengths into a strong, quilt-like fabric that is more brilliant and beautiful than the strengths of any single individual or group of similar individuals could produce, while muting and neutralizing weaknesses. A synergistic effect emerges, so that the weaknesses of some employees are complemented by the strengths of others.

Sometimes, instead of trustworthy leadership, however, we get transitional and toxic leadership. Under these treacherous leadership types, a collective dynamic also emerges, but not one that promotes the mission of the organization. Rather, the mission of the organization is diminished, progress is delayed or stalled, and much time is spent disparaging others who work for the same organization. Eventually, the organizational mission is displaced by the need to survive, and survival becomes equated with reducing and even destroying others. Under toxic leadership, the combined resources of the people working in the organization is less than the whole, for many of these resources are drained into dysfunctional strategies and games.

Transitional leaders permit the baser instincts of others to prevail, resulting in friction, conflict, individual pursuit of advantage at collective expense, and ultimately organizational dysfunction. More malicious toxic leaders actually create and exacerbate conflict and organizational dysfunctioning.

Under both transitional and toxic leadership, a similar pattern of organizational decline emerges. The decline typically occurs faster and descends further under toxic leadership than under transitional leadership, but the stages of decline are comparable under both types. Some organizations may speed through various stages, or even on rare occasion skip a stage, depending on the personalities involved and peculiarities of the setting. Most organizations, however, pass through seven stages in their downward spiral of decline and dysfunctioning. These seven stages constitute the anatomy of organizational decline.

THE ANATOMY OF ORGANIZATIONAL DECLINE

Each stage of decline has certain characteristics that make it identifiable to an outsider, although those living through decline may be so swept up in the dysfunctional games and strategies, so overcome with anxiety, and so emotionally angry or fearful that clear analysis of the stages evades them. Understanding this anatomy of organizational decline, however, helps us recognize it, analyze it, and begin to identify strategies for reversing the dysfunction and restoring organizational health.

An organization that is in stage one is still operating under *green light leadership*. At the beginning of decline, the organization is still relatively healthy, although the seeds of dysfunction in the form of present but not yet visible toxic leadership are present. A workplace that slips into stages two and three has caught the equivalent of an increasingly severe, organizational cold. It now has fallen under *yellow light leadership*. Things are bad and foreboding worse, but still relatively correctable. What is required here mostly are actions taken at the individual level to alter rewards, perceptions, and attitudes.

By the time the workplace falls to stages four and five, covert and overt warfare have emerged. By now the organization is under the influence of *red light leadership*. Such a workplace is in the throes of a major, threatening battle with guerrilla and then open warfare occurring. All pretenses of normality are eventually dropped by the end of stage five. Individual remedies are no longer an option. Only remedies involving whole groups of people will work.

An organization that has descended to stages six and seven is truly sick with a life-threatening illness. It may or may not survive in a recognizable form. The ravages of toxic leadership are readily apparent. Clients, customers, employees, suppliers, and investors all suffer. Only surgery or other drastic remedies will keep the organization alive.

Green Light Leadership Before the Descent: Transitional and Toxic Leaders Are Not Yet Evident

Stage One: Trust and Cooperation. Initially, organizations that spin into decline appear healthy. Trustworthy leadership still prevails as the flaws of toxic leadership have been masked or are not yet apparent. Employees work in an atmosphere of trust and cooperation. There is sharing of information among individuals and different divisions and groups in the organization. Different factions and groups have not yet staked out turf worth defending at increasingly higher costs. Face-to-face interactions are cordial and friendly.

Since trust is the operative mode of employees and leaders, there is no need to document every aspect of decision making. Nor is there any perceived gap between toxic leader rhetoric and reality. Initially, employees believe that the transitional or toxic leaders value the entire organization and its mission. Employees believe these leaders mean what they say with no hidden meaning, self promotion, or malicious undercurrents.

Yellow Light Leadership at the Beginning of the Descent: Transitional and Toxic Leaders Appear

Stage Two: Disappointment and Disillusionment. Transitional and toxic leaders' flaws and their impact on the organization become more apparent, although as yet, are not spoken about openly in public meetings. Employees who do not share the values of the treacherous leaders privately respond to leader dictates with disbelief and incredulity. Employees express disappointment in the performance and decisions of the transitional or toxic leader. Followers perceive a growing rhetoric/reality gap. Employees silently notice the transitional or toxic leader stating one set of values conducive to organizational health and growth, yet making decisions by and acting on a different, more self-serving set of values. These selfish values undercut organizational and employee well-being for the benefit of leader self-promotion.

As employee disillusionment and disenchantment grow, so do anxiety and skepticism. Many employees cease true sharing of information. Increasingly, they reveal information selectively and fail to mention or provide information they perceive will be used inappropriately by the treacherous leaders. As the circulation of useful information slows down, so does effective decision making. Disillusioned employees spend increasing effort checking out the validity of information provided, manipulated, issued, or filtered by the transitional or toxic leader through external sources and through one-on-one or informal, small group meetings with like-minded fellow workers.

As secretive checking and validating of information increase, indecisiveness of employees in following toxic leader mandates also increases. Self-esteem of employees begins to decrease as employees notice the consequent dipping productivity. Employees grow uncertain and anxious. The toxic leader frequently responds by becoming more harsh and issuing more mandates. This does not, however, successfully combat growing disillusionment, for with each mandate, disbelief and incredulity of employees at the toxic leader rhetoric/reality gap grows.

Stage Three: Outrage and Contempt. Employees who care about the organization become outraged at the transitional and toxic leader rhetoric/reality gap. The gap exists because transitional and toxic leaders protest rhetorically that organizational missions and goals are important but perform in reality as if only selfish and self-centered goals matter. Employees develop contempt for the transitional and toxic leaders and their supporters. As outrage and contempt supersede disillusionment and disgust, the transitional and toxic leaders become less and less effective in achieving any goals, even personally aggrandizing ones. The organization begins to break up into factions, with the common break occurring between supporters and opponents of the toxic leader. Each side begins to characterize the other as being out for self interest and making decisions strictly on the basis of personal gain.

The transitional and toxic leaders begin to use meetings as a control mechanism. The real intent of the meetings is to smash dissent before it can coalesce, but if this fails, the contempt of some opponents is barely concealed and increasingly visible. The meandering meetings exacerbate organizational decline rather than reduce it, by forcing employees that disagree with each other to interact more frequently in settings where the disagreements will likely become apparent.

The obviousness of the differences and of the leaders' flaws, including the rhetoric/reality gap, augment the outrage and contempt of transitional and toxic leader opponents. Throughout stage three, however, organizational factions remain fluid, with individuals not positive how others feel, nor sure to what degree others share their views.

Red Light Leadership in the Descent: Toxic Leaders Dominate

Stage Four: Covert Game Playing. The factions that began to develop in stage three are solidified. Members of each side continue to disguise and conceal true motives from the opposing faction, but no longer from each other. Secret meetings of factions to compare notes, strategize, and discuss options become customary. Members of opposing factions, especially those associated with the toxic leader's faction, become deceitful, by stating irrelevant or inaccurate rationales for personal actions. Self-aggrandizing proposals are presented as beneficial to the organization and its mission. All faction members begin to reinterpret the statements of opponents to assess true rationales, recognizing they may bear little resemblance to and cover up true rationales.

First, the toxic leader, and then others begin to overemphasize personal achievement, and private and public criticisms of members of opposing factions become customary. The toxic leader's possessiveness of functions and duties extends to others, who become protective of their organizational turf. Meetings become numerous and develop into combat zones in which lateral attacks and guerilla skirmishes take place. Toxic leaders continue to attempt to use meetings as control devices. Absences from meetings, even for legitimate reasons, become black marks on employee records and are interpreted as signs of disloyalty.

Since the real purpose of most meetings is toxic leader control and smashing dissent, meetings often meander sullenly and then race rapidly, with the contents having little relationship to the stated agenda, if there was one. Complex measures and major policy changes are proposed with no forewarning and no chance for opponents to study them in their entirety if at all. Surprise becomes a key element for the success of proposals dealing with turf protection and expansion. Subordinates of the toxic leader become afraid to miss meetings for fear of what will be enacted behind their backs.

Yet as combat between factions becomes the main focus of meetings, and many proposals are put forth without consensus or rationale, little attention is devoted to policy enforcement and follow through. When enforcement does occur, it is selective, arbitrary, and designed to enhance the toxic leader's power or reduce the power of opponents, rather than linked to any strategy of organizational growth. Rules and regulations become tools in the hands of toxic leaders. Opponents begin to similarly rely on rules and regulations for protection.

Stage Five: Open Warfare. In stage five, covertness and pretense are dropped as relations become more hostile. Open warfare between the toxic leader and his opponents breaks out. More and more employees are dragged into the fray as the organizational conflict spills into the open and becomes heated, just as innocent bystanders are dragged unwillingly into war. Fewer and fewer employees are able to maintain the neutral "Switzerland" role as innocent actions are interpreted by the toxic leader as signs of disloyalty or by the opponents as signs of toxic leader support.

Members of factions publicly and privately discredit and disparage each other. The toxic leader attempts (and often succeeds at least temporarily) to take resources away from opposing factions. Strategizing and struggling over resources intensifies. No resource is immune from battle, even the lowly xerox machine, which the toxic leader often seizes. Computers and other communications networks are sources of big battles, as are organizational pots of money. The toxic leader attempts to control opponent travel and to limit contact between geographically disperse opponents to prevent further coalescence.

Attacks become overt, frontal, and personal as the toxic leader becomes vindictive. Charges of incompetence are common. The toxic leader begins to use annual and periodic evaluations of subordinates as weapons to squelch dissent. Favorable evaluations, raises, and other resources are distributed on the basis of loyalty to the toxic leader. Threats of grievances and formal complaints ensue. Total preoccupation with organizational conflict emerges, and each faction goes outside of channels to report misdeeds to superiors. All organizational actions and behaviors are now interpreted through the filter of toxic leader/opponent conflict.

The Bottom: The Impact of Toxic Leaders

Stage Six: Siege Mentality. In stage six, a siege mentality develops, especially on the part of employees who seem to be losing power. Normal practices and norms are violated. Lines of authority are breached as both the toxic leader and opponents appeal to higher levels, if the toxic leader does not head up the entire organization.

The losing faction broadens the conflict by soliciting the advice and support of outsiders and bystanders. Outsiders are brought into the conflict, often involuntarily and even when their involvement is inappropriate and unethical. At this point, customers, clients, suppliers, consultants, and tangentially linked persons are involved by one or another faction. The toxic leader may threaten to involve the courts and sue opponents for personal defamation or for unspecified reasons. Each faction threatens and may achieve formal investigations of opponents.

Factions and key players see no hope for alleviating the conflict, no possible good in the actions and motives of the other side, and no solution for the turmoil. Paranoia reigns. Members of one or the other faction, especially the toxic leader, feel that opponents have unfair influence on and over the now involved players from outside the unit. Productivity almost screeches to a halt. Rumors of trouble and turmoil spread beyond the organization, making outsiders leery of working in it or being associated with it.

Stage Seven: Isolation and Alienation. If the toxic leader is not removed, deposed, or driven away from the organization, opponents of the toxic leader become isolated and alienated in stage seven. Yet all employees, battle worn and scarred, experience emotional exhaustion. Hopelessness and cynicism prevail. Many subordinates withdraw completely and emotionally from work and cease caring about the organization. Now thoroughly cynical and emotionally devastated, employees minimize the effort and time spent on their jobs to reduce the pain association and intense involvement which work has brought them. Skepticism of outsiders who have been dragged into the conflict or who have heard about the troubled organization reinforces internal disarray and despair.

Communication channels break down almost totally between the toxic leader and those alienated. Subordinates, and particularly opponents who are different from the toxic leader in race, sex, professional training, or other key characteristics, are most likely to be isolated first. Meetings that were once highly charged and frequent events in earlier stages are poorly attended. Toxic leader memos are ignored. Requests for transfers within the organization and applications for jobs elsewhere rise into a torrent. Opponents of the toxic leader who can leave the organization do so. Even some earlier supporters, disgusted by the extreme and malicious tactics the toxic leader may have used in later stages to retain control, are exhausted and seek to leave.

Employees who cannot leave withdraw emotionally and barely endure; productivity plummets further and organizational performance declines to new lows. Whether the organization survives such precipitous productivity drops depends on how protracted the conflict was, how extreme the toxic leader's tactics were, and how harsh the current economic environment is that the organization confronts.

The consequences of a cycle of organizational decline are devastating. Consider the impact Ross Johnson, CEO of RJR Nabisco, had on that organization. Johnson, a high-living hedonist, secretly planned to buy out the company in 1988 in a maneuver Bryan Burrough and John Helyar call "the ultimate story of greed and glory."[1] The displays of egos by Ross and others were so brazen as to be unparalleled in American business since the gilded age. The driving force behind the machinations that Johnson's attempt at a leveraged buyout spun into motion was "true greed."[2] Ross was described as free-wheeling and free-spending and out of synch with the pinstripe culture of RJR Nabisco. Factions pro and con Johnson already existed in the company from the previous uneasy merger of R. J. Reynolds (RJR), the tobacco giant, and Nabisco, the food company, from which Johnson had emerged. Ultimately his maneuvers prompted Henry Kravis of Kohlberg, Kravis, Roberts and Co. (KKR) to enter into the fray and win the battle for the company by a KKR buyout of RJR Nabisco. But in the process of fighting between the financial giant and the recklessly spending CEO, the company slipped into decline, with uncertainty increasing, morale plummeting, and despair growing. Only the subsequent departure of Johnson, who lost the battle to KKR, began to restore the company's morale and health.

Similar loss of morale occurred in the besieged Nixon White House during Watergate. The episode was eventually characterized as "a cancer on the presidency," and spawned disagreement over what should be done.[3] Factions developed over whether and how big a cover-up should occur, whether the president should "take the heat," and ultimately, who was to blame for the illegal events that occurred. Again, morale plummeted, normal functioning became onerous, and ultimately, trusted enforcers Bob Haldeman, John Ehrlichman, and John Dean were fired. Those that left and those that stayed scrambled to find cover for themselves, eventually abandoning any hope of carrying out their formal duties. Only the removal of Nixon by his resignation and his replacement in the presidency with Gerald Ford began the recovery process, both in White House functioning and the national psyche.

NOTES

1. Bryan Burrough and John Helyar, *Barbarians at the Gate: The Fall of RJR Nabisco* (New York: Harper and Row, 1990), pp. 1–9.

2. Hope Lampert, *True Greed: What Really Happened in the Battle for RJR Nabisco* (New York: New American Library, 1990), p. 1.

3. Stephen E. Ambrose, *Nixon*, vol. 3, *Ruin and Recovery 1973–1990* (New York: Simon and Schuster, 1991), pp. 81–136.

13

Regaining
Organizational Health

TURNING ORGANIZATIONS AROUND

What can be done about organizations who have been driven into decline by transitional and toxic leaders? Must organizations that start on the downhill slide into decline go through all the stages to hit rock bottom? What happens then if they do?

Several strategies can be used to halt and reverse organizational decline. The strategies may be ranked in terms of impact on the organization itself and on its employees. The strategy with the least impact is expanding the organizational resource base. The second least severe strategy for most employees in the organization is removing the toxic leader. The third strategy in terms of gravity and size of impact is restructuring the organization. The most severe strategy with the greatest impact is abolishing the organization.

Which strategy is appropriate? The answer depends on the following factors:

1. *How long the decline has gone on.* If decline has persisted for a long time, then dysfunctional behaviors have become habitual and are deeply ingrained. More severe strategies will be needed to reverse long-standing behavior patterns.

2. *How far the decline has proceeded.* The more stages of decline through which the organization has passed, the more severe the strategy that will be needed to successfully combat organizational dysfunction. An organization that has begun to dysfunction will not necessarily go through all the stages and hit rock bottom, but the further down

the organization has slid, the more severe the strategy that will be needed to pull it out of malaise and to restore productivity.

3. *How many transitional and toxic leaders there are.* If an organization has only one or two transitional or toxic leaders that are creating havoc with their behavior and making the organization dysfunctional, then less severe strategies to combat decline may be adequate. If, however, the organization has many transitional and toxic leaders, more severe strategies are needed.

   If decline has persisted for sometime, the likelihood is great that the number of toxic leaders will increase, for toxic leaders attract each other. Trustworthy leaders drive toxic leaders out, by virtue of acting on a higher moral plane and maintaining high standards of productivity. Toxic leaders, however, benefit from and feed off of each other's dysfunctional behavior.

4. *Where the toxic leaders are located within the organization.* Are transitional and toxic leaders layered in several successive levels in the organizational hierarchy, or are they dispersed? If toxic leaders are layered, severe strategies are needed. Merely removing one toxic leader will not solve the problem of organizational dysfunction when toxic leaders are several layers deep. Remaining toxic leaders will work to see that the replacement is no better than the one who was removed.

   Even if a trustworthy leader is selected, he will immediately be stifled and attacked by threatened toxic leaders who have observed one of their own be stripped of authority. If, however, the toxic leaders are relatively dispersed and can be organizationally isolated, less severe remedies may work.

STRATEGIES FOR COUNTERING YELLOW LIGHT LEADERSHIP

Several strategies may be used to counter and combat organizational decline. Each has advantages and disadvantages. The first two strategies for countering organizational decline—expanding the organizational resource base and removing the transitional or toxic leader—may be sufficient to correct yellow light leadership.

Expanding the Organizational Resource Base. This strategy involves giving dysfunctional units more resources in an attempt to mitigate the infighting that invariably becomes worse when resources are tight. Thus, toxic leaders and their factions are bought off by giving them less reason to fight and by making them feel relatively successful and more secure.

This strategy is more likely to be employed in times of economic plenty than in times of economic scarcity, so its actual use may depend as much on conditions external to the organization as those internal to it. Expanding the resource base as a strategy for combating decline has the advantage of leaving organizational arrangements intact, thereby avoiding the turmoil that results if organizational arrangements are changed.

This strategy also has several major disadvantages. It rewards units that by their dysfunction have been less productive, sending a message to other units and organizations that the way to get more resources is to fight internally rather than to produce more. It may actually increase the power of the transitional or toxic leader by giving him more resources with which to reward supporters and penalize opponents. Thus it may not work. Finally, it may not be a rational, efficient allocation of resources overall.

Removing the Transitional or Toxic Leader. This strategy entails removing the transitional or toxic leader from his position of authority. The toxic leader may either be forced out of the organization, or forced into a peripheral role that does not affect the whole organization. This strategy has the advantage of removing the immediate problem and source of decline.

Moving the transitional or toxic leader into a lesser role also has disadvantages. If the leader is not forced out of the organization, and in some settings this may not be possible or even desirable, the disgruntled and angry transitional or toxic leader may become a destructive force, even without formal power, sabotaging whenever possible all efforts to restore the organization to health. If decline is quite advanced, then the bitterness from infighting may not be addressed or solved merely by replacing the toxic leader.

But the most crucial problem, since most removed toxic leaders can be neutralized to some degree, is finding an adequate replacement for the toxic leader. If economic conditions are harsh, then recruitment of a replacement from outside the organization may be hampered or not possible. If recruitment must occur internally, then the toxic leader has probably trained no one to replace him, and has worked hard, in fact, to assure the reverse. If decline is severe, most likely the toxic leader has already attracted other toxic leaders, limiting the pool of trustworthy leaders available internally.

STRATEGIES FOR COUNTERING RED LIGHT LEADERSHIP

The third and fourth strategies for countering and combatting organization decline—restructuring the organization and abolishing the organization—are far more drastic, but may be necessary to restore productivity and eventual organizational health.

Restructuring the Organization. This option is more severe than merely replacing the toxic leader. It involves everyone in the organization. Dysfunctional units are restructured: the dysfunctional unit may be merged with more healthy units; pieces may be removed and shifted to other divisions; while other pieces may be combined in an attempt to mitigate infighting and neutralize toxic leaders. In the process one or more toxic leaders in the unit may have their authority reduced, or they may be replaced. The unit continues as a whole, but looks very different.

This strategy is more likely to work as an antidote to organizational decline with a bigger unit. The bigger the unit, the greater the flexibility for restructuring, and the greater the likelihood that trustworthy leadership talent that can assume control exists within the unit. It is less likely to work for small units and organizations, for there are few logical options for restructuring subunits into new combinations.

This strategy has the advantage of retaining the organization's identity. Organizations across time tend to take on a life of their own, and do not die easily, even when afflicted with the virus of toxic leadership and showing the sickness of organizational decline. Even if organizational health is eventually restored by restructuring, the new structure may not initially increase productivity. Productivity increases may take some time to materialize and may do so only after new working arrangements are established. Restoring employee self-esteem and allowing for development of skills of employees who have not had such opportunities or who have been discouraged from taking advantage of such opportunities will also take time.

Abolishing the Organization. In the most extreme cases of decline, the only feasible option may be to abolish the organization. If the dysfunction is occurring in a division within a larger organization, pieces of the organization may be split up and spun off to other healthier divisions. If the whole organization is sick, pieces may be sold in the private sector. In the public sector, pieces may be moved to other departments or agencies. In some instances, the whole organization may be swallowed up by a larger organization, as in the case of mergers and hostile takeovers.

The most extreme is to disband the organization totally. This happens in cases of bankruptcy in the private sector, colleges that shut down, and abandonment of public sector agencies. While ostensibly the reason for some of these organizational abolitions is economic, each likely experienced a preceding period of organizational decline.

RESTORING GREEN LIGHT LEADERSHIP

How might organizations stay healthy in the future and prevent the agony and ultimate defeat of toxic leadership? Both the process of decline and the remedies for correcting it are painful, and if both could be avoided, then everyone associated with an organization, as well as the economy as a whole, would be better off. Are there any preventive strategies? Strategies to prevent decline are easier to discuss than to implement. Following are some personal actions that may help you prevent decline or survive it, if prevention is not possible:

1. Be aware that toxic leadership is a real threat to organizational health, and be vigilant for the first signs of it.

2. Talk with transitional and toxic leaders in as non-threatening a fashion as possible when they first start exhibiting dysfunctional behavior and let them know you are aware of what they are doing.

3. If transitional and toxic leaders continue to act dysfunctionally, start through the organizational hierarchy, following appropriate chains of command, expressing concerns about what is going on.

4. Put everything in writing, as later you may need documentation.

5. Try to identify trustworthy leaders who are genuinely concerned about the health of the organization and the welfare of its employees. Reach out to these leaders with your concerns.

6. Be firm at every step, refusing to engage in dysfunctional behavior just because others are doing it.

7. Try to maintain productivity despite efforts of others to undermine it. Bring collective attention back to productivity at every possible juncture.

8. Take a long-run view about petty slights and actions, ignoring them whenever possible.

9. Refuse to participate in secret meetings and agreements that cannot be revealed publicly, for closed environments are a part of creating a culture of decline.

10. Remember that toxic leaders are fundamentally flawed and will eventually self-destruct. Organizational decline, like any sickness, is dynamic, not static. A sick organization will eventually get better or die. In either event, toxic leaders will be replaced.

The greatest antidote to toxic leadership and the organizational decline it foments is trustworthy leadership. We should seek out trustworthy leaders, encourage and support them when we find them, and seek to become them. They are our greatest hope for healthy productive workplaces.

References

Abbott, Philip. *The Exemplary Presidency: Franklin Roosevelt and the American Political Tradition.* Amherst: University of Massachusetts Press, 1990.

Abodaher, David. *Iacocca.* New York: Macmillan, 1982.

Adams, John D., ed. *Transforming Leadership: From Vision to Results.* Alexandria, VA: Miles River Press, 1986.

Ambrose, Stephen E. *Nixon.* vol. 3, *Ruin and Recovery 1973–1990.* New York: Simon and Schuster, 1991.

Anderson, Jack, and Ronald W. May. *McCarthy: The Man, the Senator, and the "Ism."* Boston: Beacon Press, 1952.

Argyris, Chris. "Productive and Counter-Productive Reasoning Processes." In *The Executive Mind*, ed. Suresh Srivastva and Associates. San Francisco: Jossey-Bass, 1983.

Badaracco, Joseph L., Jr., and Richard R. Ellsworth. *Leadership and the Quest for Integrity.* Boston: Harvard Business School Press, 1989.

Barge, J. Kevin. *Leadership: Communication Skills for Organizations and Groups.* New York: St. Martin's Press, 1994.

Barry, John, with Tony Clifton, Daniel Pedersen, Christopher Dickey, Ruth Marshall, Theodore Stranger, Fred Colman, Michael Meyer, John McCormick, Ginny Carroll, and Donna Foote. "Making of a Myth: The October Surprise." *Newsweek*, November 11, 1991: 18–25.

Beer, Michael, Russell A. Eisenstat, and Bert Spector. *The Critical Path to Corporate Renewal.* Boston: Harvard Business School Press, 1990.

Bennis, Warren. *On Becoming a Leader.* Reading, MA: Addison-Wesley, 1994.

Bennis, Warren, and Burt Nanus. *Leaders: The Strategies for Taking Charge.* New York: Harper and Row, 1985.

Berman, Larry, and Bruce W. Jentleson. "Bush and the Post–Cold War World: New Challenges for American Leadership." In *Bush Presidency: First Appraisals*, ed. Colin Campbell and Bert A. Rockman. Chatham, NJ: Chatham House, 1991.

Beschloss, Michael R., and Strobe Talbott. *At the Highest Levels: The Inside Story of the End of the Cold War.* Boston: Little, Brown, 1993.

Bing, Stanley. *Crazy Bosses: Spotting Them, Serving Them, and Surviving Them*. New York: William Morrow, 1992.

Blum, Howard. *Gangland: How the FBI Broke the Mob*. New York: Simon and Schuster, 1993.

Borger, Gloria, and Jerry Buckley with David Gergen, Steven V. Roberts, Dorian Friedman, and Bureau Reports. "Perot Keeps Going and Going . . . ." *U.S. News and World Reports* 114, no. 19 (May 17, 1993): 37–47.

Bradlee, Ben, Jr. *Guts and Glory: The Rise and Fall of Oliver North*. New York: Donald I. Fine, 1988.

Bruck, Connie. *The Predators' Ball: The Junk-Bond Raiders and the Man Who Staked Them*. New York: Simon and Schuster, 1988.

Bullock, Alan. *Hitler: A Study in Tyranny*. Rev. ed. New York: Harper and Row, 1962.

Burke, John P., and Fred I. Greenstein, with Larry Berman and Richard Immerman. *How Presidents Test Reality: Decisions on Vietnam, 1954 and 1965*. New York: Russell Sage Foundation, 1989.

Burns, James MacGregor. *Leadership*. New York: Harper and Row, 1978.

Burns, James MacGregor. *Roosevelt: The Lion and the Fox*. Vol. 1. Norwalk, CT: Easton Press, 1956.

Burns, James MacGregor. *Roosevelt: The Soldier of Freedom*. Vol. 2. Norwalk, CT: Easton Press, 1970.

Burrough, Bryan, and John Helyar. *Barbarians at the Gate: The Fall of RJR Nabisco*. New York: Harper and Row, 1990.

Cannon, Lou. *President Reagan: The Role of a Lifetime*. New York: Simon and Schuster, 1991.

Carlson, Jody. *George C. Wallace and the Politics of Powerlessness: The Wallace Campaigns for the Presidency, 1964–1976*. New Brunswick, NJ: Transaction Books, 1981.

Caro, Robert A. *Means of Ascent: The Years of Lyndon Johnson*. New York: Alfred A. Knopf, 1990.

Caro, Robert A. *The Path to Power: The Years of Lyndon Johnson*. New York: Alfred A. Knopf, 1982.

Carter, Jay. *Nasty People: How to Stop Being Hurt by Them Without Becoming One of Them*. Chicago: Contemporary Books, 1989.

Chesen, Eli S. *President Nixon's Psychiatric Profile: A Psychodynamic-Genetic Interpretation*. New York: Peter H. Wyden, 1973.

Chidester, David. *Salvation and Suicide: An Interpretation of Jim Jones, the Peoples Temple, and Jonestown*. Bloomington: Indiana University Press, 1988.

"C.I.A.'s Casey Departs from Practice in Keeping Control of His Own Stocks." *New York Times*, November 23, 1981, p. A16.

Cronin, Thomas E. "Reflections on Leadership." In *Contemporary Issues in Leadership*, ed. William E. Rosenbach and Robert L. Taylor. 3rd ed. Bouldor, CO: Westview Press, 1993.

Dallek, Robert. *Lone Star Rising: Lyndon Johnson and His Times: 1908–1960*. New York: Oxford University Press, 1991.

Dean, John W., III. *Blind Ambition: The White House Years*. New York: Simon and Schuster, 1976.

DeGregorio, William A. *The Complete Book of U.S. Presidents*. 3rd ed. New York: Wings Books, 1991.

Demaris, Ovid. *The Director: An Oral Biography of J. Edgar Hoover*. New York: Harper's Magazine Press, 1975.

Dietrich, Noah, and Bob Thomas. *Howard: The Amazing Mr. Hughes.* Greenwich, CT: Fawcett Publications, 1972.

Dietrich, Otto. *Hitler.* Translated by Richard and Clara Winston. Chicago: Henry Regnery, 1953.

Downs, Anthony. *Inside Bureaucracy.* Boston: Little, Brown, 1967.

Drew, Elizabeth. *Washington Journal: The Events of 1973–1974.* New York: Random House, 1975.

Drosnin, Michael. *Citizen Hughes.* New York: Holt, Rinehart, and Winston, 1985.

Dugger, Ronnie. *The Politician: The Life and Times of Lyndon Johnson—The Drive for Power, from the Frontier to Master of the Senate.* New York: W. W. Norton, 1982.

Elgin, Suzette Haden. *Success with the Gentle Art of Verbal Self-Defense.* Englewood Cliffs, NJ: Prentice-Hall, 1989.

Feuerlicht, Roberta Strauss. *Joe McCarthy and McCarthyism: The Hate that Haunts America.* New York: McGraw-Hill, 1972.

Fiedler, Fred E., and Joseph E. Garcia. *New Approaches to Effective Leadership: Cognitive Resources and Organizational Performance.* New York: John Wiley & Sons, 1987.

Frady, Marshall. *Wallace.* New York: The World, 1968.

Friedlander, Frank. "Patterns of Individual and Organizational Learning." In *The Executive Mind,* ed. Suresh Srivastva and Associates. San Francisco: Jossey-Bass, 1983.

Garrow, David J. *The FBI and Martin Luther King, Jr.: From "Solo" to Memphis.* New York: W. W. Norton, 1981.

Gordon, Maynard M. *The Iacocca Management Technique.* New York: Dodd, Mead, 1985.

Griffith, Robert. *The Politics of Fear: Joseph R. McCarthy and the Senate.* 2nd ed. Amherst: University of Massachusetts Press, 1987.

Hall, John R. *Gone from the Promised Land: Jonestown in American Cultural History.* New Brunswick, NJ: Transaction Books, 1987.

Hitler, Adolf, *Mein Kampf.* Translated by James Murphy. London: Hurst & Blackett, 1939.

Hitt, William D. *Ethics and Leadership: Putting Theory into Practice.* Columbus, OH: Battelle Press, 1990.

Hurt, Harry, III. *Lost Tycoon: The Many Lives of Donald J. Trump.* New York: W. W. Norton, 1993.

Jaap, Tom. *Enabling Leadership: Achieving Results with People.* 2nd ed. Brookfield, VT: Gower, 1989.

Jaffen, Dennis T., Cynthia D. Scott, and Esther M. Orioli. "Visionary Leadership: Moving a Company from Burnout to Inspired Performance." In *Transforming Leadership: From Vision To Results,* ed. John D. Adams. Alexandria, VA: Miles River Press, 1986.

Jaques, Elliot, and Stephen D. Clement. *Executive Leadership: A Practical Guide to Managing Complexity.* Cambridge, MA: Basil Blackwell, 1991.

Jewell, Malcolm E., and Marcia Lynn Whicker. *Legislative Leadership in the American States.* Ann Arbor: University of Michigan Press, 1994.

Johnson, Haynes. *Sleepwalking Through History: America in the Reagan Years.* New York: W. W. Norton, 1991.

Jones, Bryan D., ed. *Leadership and Politics: New Perspectives in Political Science.* Lawrence: University of Kansas Press, 1989.

Kearns, Doris. *Lyndon Johnson and the American Dream.* New York: Harper and Row, 1976.

Kets de Vries, Manfred F. R., ed. *The Irrational Executive: Psychoanalytic Explorations in Management.* New York: International Universities Press, 1984.

Kets de Vries, Manfred F. R., and Danny Miller. *The Neurotic Organization.* San Francisco: Jossey-Bass, 1984.

Kets de Vries, Manfred F. R., and Danny Miller. *Unstable at the Top: Inside the Troubled Organization.* New York: New American Library, 1987.

Koestenbaum, Peter. *Leadership: The Inner Side of Greatness.* San Francisco: Jossey-Bass, 1991.

Kornbluth, Jesse. *Highly Confident: The Crime and Punishment of Michael Milken.* New York: William Morrow, 1992.

Kotter, John P. *A Force for Change: How Leadership Differs from Management.* New York: Free Press, 1990.

Kouzes, James M., and Barry Z. Posner. "The Credibility Factor: What People Expect of Leaders." In *Contemporary Issues in Leadership.* 3rd ed. Boulder, CO: Westview Press, 1993.

Lampert, Hope. *True Greed: What Really Happened in the Battle for RJR Nabisco.* New York: New American Library, 1990.

Levin, Doron P. *Irreconcilable Differences: Perot Versus General Motors.* Boston: Little, Brown, 1989.

Lukas, J. Anthony. *Nightmare: The Underside of the Nixon Years.* New York: Viking Press, 1976.

Maccoby, Michael. *The Gamesman: Winning and Losing the Career Game.* New York: Bantam, 1976.

MacGregor, Douglas. "The Human Side of Enterprise." *Management Review* 46 (1957): 22–28.

Maslow, Abraham. *Motivation and Personality.* New York: Harper and Row, 1954.

Mason, Todd. *Perot: An Unauthorized Biography.* Homewood, IL: Dow Jones-Irwin, 1990.

Mastenbroek, Willem F. G. *Conflict Management and Organizational Development.* New York: John Wiley, 1987.

McClelland, David C. *The Achieving Society.* Princeton, NJ: D. Van Nostrand, 1961.

Mintzberg, Henry, and James A. Waters. "The Mind of the Strategist(s)." In *The Executive Mind,* ed. Suresh Srivastva and Associates. San Francisco: Jossey-Bass, 1983.

Neustadt, Richard. *Presidential Power.* New York: John Wiley, 1960.

North, Oliver, with William Novak. *Under Fire: An American Story.* New York: HarperCollins, 1991.

O'Reilly, Kenneth. *Hoover and the Un-Americans: The FBI, HUAC, and the Red Menace.* Philadelphia: Temple University Press, 1983.

Ouchi, William G. *Theory Z: How American Business Can Meet the Japanese Challenge.* New York: Avon Books, 1981.

Passell, Peter. "America's Position in the Economic Race: What the Numbers Show and Conceal." *New York Times,* March 4, 1990, pp. A4–A5.

Persico, Joseph E. *Casey: From the OSS to the CIA.* New York: Viking, 1990.

Pondy, Louis R. "Union of Rationality and Intuition." In *The Executive Mind,* ed. Suresh Srivastva and Associates. San Francisco: Jossey-Bass, 1983.

Reagan, Ronald. *An American Life.* New York: Simon and Schuster, 1990.

Reed, Harold W. *The Dynamics of Leadership.* Danville, IL: The Interstate, 1982.

Regan, Donald T. *For the Record: From Wall Street to Washington.* San Diego, CA: Harcourt Brace Jovanovich, 1988.

Reiterman, Tim, with John Jacobs. *Raven: The Untold Story of the Reverend Jim Jones and His People.* New York: E. P. Dutton, 1982.

Reston, James, Jr., *Our Father Who Art in Hell.* New York: Times Books, 1981.

Robert, Michael. *The Essence of Leadership: Strategy, Innovation, and Decisiveness.* New York: Quorum, 1991.

Roberts, Wess. *Leadership Secrets of Attila the Hun.* New York: Warner Books, 1990.

Rorty, James, and Moshe Decter. *McCarthy and the Communists.* Boston: Beacon Press, 1954.

Rosenback, William E., and Robert L. Taylor, eds. *Contemporary Issues in Leadership.* 2nd ed. Boulder, CO: Westview Press, 1989.

Rost, Joseph C. *Leadership for the Twenty-First Century.* Westport, CT: Greenwood Press, 1991.

Scott, W. Richard. *Organizations: Rational, Natural, and Open Systems.* 2nd ed. Englewood Cliffs, NJ: Prentice-Hall, 1987.

Serling, Robert. *Howard Hughes' Airline: An Informal History of TWA.* New York: St. Martin's, 1983.

Sheehy, Gail. *Character: America's Search for Leadership.* New York: William Morrow, 1988.

Sims, Henry P., Jr., and Peter Lorenzi. *The New Leadership Paradigm: Social Learning and Cognition in Organizations.* Newbury Park, CA: Sage Publications, 1992.

Spencer, Scott. "Lawrence Walsh's Last Battle." *New York Times Magazine* (July 4, 1993): 11, 28–33.

Srivasta, Suresh and Associates, eds. *The Executive Mind.* San Francisco: Jossey-Bass, 1983.

Stein, Benjamin J. *A License to Steal: The Untold Story of Michael Milken and the Conspiracy to Bilk the Nation.* New York: Simon and Schuster, 1992.

Stoakes, Geoffrey. *Hitler and the Quest for World Domination.* New York: St. Martin's Press, 1986.

Stone, Dan G. *April Fools: An Insider's Account of the Rise and Collapse of Drexel Burnham.* New York: Donald I. Fine, 1990.

Strebel, Paul. *Breakpoints: How Managers Exploit Radical Business Change.* Boston: Harvard Business School Press, 1990.

Stuckey, Mary E., and Frederick J. Antczak. "Governance as Political Theater: George Bush and the MTV Presidency." In *Leadership and the Bush Presidency: Prudence or Drift in an Era of Change?* ed. Ryan J. Barilleaux and Mary E. Stuckey. Westport, CT: Praeger, 1992.

Summers, Anthony. *Official and Confidential: The Secret Life of J. Edgar Hoover.* New York: G. P. Putnam's Sons, 1993.

Theoharis, Athan G., and John Stuart Cox. *The Boss: J. Edgar Hoover and the Great American Inquisition.* Philadelphia: Temple University Press, 1988.

Thomas, Lately. *When Angels Wept: The Senator Joseph McCarthy Affair: A Story Without a Hero.* William Morrow, 1973.

Thomas, Tony. *Howard Hughes in Hollywood.* Secaucus, NJ: Citadel, 1985.

Thurow, Lester. Speech given at Midlands Technical College, Columbia, SC, March 1986.

Tichy, Noel M., and Mary Anne Devanna. *The Transformational Leader.* New York: John Wiley & Sons, 1986.

Torbert, Robert R. "Cultivating Timely Executive Action." In *The Executive Mind,* ed. Suresh Srivastva and Associates. San Francisco: Jossey-Bass, 1983.

Trump, Donald J., with Tony Schwartz. *Trump: The Art of the Deal.* New York: Random House, 1987.

Trump, Donald J., with Charles Leerhsen. *Trump: Surviving at the Top.* New York: Random House, 1990.

Tuccile, Jerome. *Trump: The Saga of America's Most Powerful Real Estate Baron.* New York: Donald I. Fine, 1985.

Tugwell, Rexford G. *The Democratic Roosevelt.* Garden City, NY: Doubleday, 1957.

Voorhis, Jerry. *The Strange Case of Richard Milhous Nixon.* New York: Paul S. Eriksson, 1972.

Wallace, George C. *Stand Up for America.* Garden City, NY: Doubleday, 1976.

Walters, J. Donald. *The Art of Supportive Leadership.* Nevada City, CA: Crystal Clarity, 1987.

Ward, Geoffrey C. *A First-Class Temperament: The Emergence of Franklin Roosevelt.* New York: Harper and Row, 1989.

Weber, Max. *The Theory of Social and Economic Organization.* New York: Free Press, 1964.

Weick, Karle E. "Managerial Thought in the Context of Action." In *The Executive Mind*, ed. Suresh Srivastva and Associates. San Francisco: Jossey-Bass, 1983.

Weightman, Judith Mary. *Making Sense of the Jonestown Suicides.* New York: Edwin Mellen Press, 1983.

Weisberg, Jacob. "Dies Ira." *New Republic* 210, no. 4 (January 24, 1994): 18–24.

Weiss, Philip. "Oliver North's Next War." *New York Times Magazine* (July 4, 1993): 12–15, 33–37.

Whicker, Marcia Lynn. "Managing and Organizing the Reagan White House." In *The Reagan Presidency: An Incomplete Revolution?* Ed. Dilys M. Hill, Raymond A. Moore, and Phil Williams. London: Macmillan, 1990.

Whicker, Marcia Lynn. "Recruitment Decision Strategies in Public Organizations: A Markhov Analysis." *Management Science and Policy Analysis* 5, no. 1 (Summer/Fall, 1987): 64–83.

Whicker, Marcia Lynn, and Jennie Jacobs Kronenfeld. "Leadership Training Models in America." *Free Inquiry in Creative Sociology* 15, no. 1 (May 1987): 35–39.

Whicker, Marcia Lynn, and Raymond A. Moore. *When Presidents Are Great.* Englewood Cliffs, NJ: Prentice-Hall, 1988.

Wicker, Tom. *One of Us: Richard Nixon and the American Dream.* New York: Random House, 1991.

Wills, Gary. "What Makes a Good Leader?" *The Atlantic Monthly* (April 1994): 63–80.

Woodward, Bob. "Casey Found to have 'Misrepresented' Facts to Win Aid for Contras." *Washington Post*, November 19, 1987.

Wyden, Peter. *The Unknown Iacocca.* New York: William Morrow, 1987.

Yukl, Gary A. *Leadership in Organizations.* 2nd ed. Englewood Cliffs, NJ: Prentice-Hall, 1989.

Index

ABOUT THE AUTHOR

MARCIA LYNN WHICKER is Chair and Professor in the Graduate Department of Public Administration, Rutgers University. Dr. Whicker has taught at Virginia Commonwealth University, University of South Carolina, Temple University, and Wayne State University, and has also worked for various government agencies. She has published thirteen books and numerous scholarly articles in the fields of leadership, public administration, public policy, and American national politics.